16N68: MY STORY

Hester Johnson Moore

16N68: MY STORY

Copyright © 2020 by Hester Johnson Moore

StoriesByHMoore@gmail.com

www.facebook.com/hester.moore.547

This book is a work of non-fiction. It is my experience as a young person leading up to, living through and trying to make sense of the events of the Memphis Sanitation Workers Strike and the devastating activities that followed. The names of some have been changed to protect their identity.

SECOND EDITION

All rights reserved. No portion of this book may be reproduced, stored in a retrieval system, or transmitted in any form or by any means – electronic, mechanical, photocopy, recording, scanning, or other – except for brief quotations in critical review or articles, without prior written permission from the author.

Cover Design & Layout: Liz Lawless

Printed in the United States of America

Printed and Distributed by Adriel Publishing

ISBN 978-1-7365239-0-2

DEDICATION
My Brother Jerry, RIP

I watched you early on when I was a child. You were like the Piped Piper. Children followed you along the way as you walked to Kansas Street Park; clinging to you like bees to honey. I knew then that you were someone Great. You had the ability to save students from themselves. You had the ability to make men out of boys. You gave and gave, whether it was your time, rides, clothes, discipline, money or advice. We are all better for it.

You loved your community. You loved your family: Pam, Lil Jerry, Jor' Don and granddaughter Emoree. You will be greatly missed.

My story is in honor of:

**Mr. William McGee
1906-1986
Sanitation Worker
1956-1974**

Husband to Hazel, Father to James, Wilma Roy, JoAnn and Darnell McGee

My life was changed the day I saw you walking home begrudgingly. I knew then I wanted to help the Sanitation Workers. Mr. McGee's earnings were $2.89 per hour at his retirement in 1974. Mr. McGee, I thank you for having the courage and grace to **Stand Tall.**

Foreword

Every year, on January 15th, Dr. King's birthday and the national holiday, and on April 4th, the assassination date of Dr. King, I reflect on the impact that the Sanitation Workers Strike in Memphis, Tennessee, Dr. King, and the Southern Christian Leadership Conference (SCLC), had on me at the tender age of 15. It is through these *reflections* that I am proud that my friend Hester wrote **16N68: My Story.**

Even at that age of 15, in 1968, I could relate to the sanitation workers desire to be recognized as men and not boys, or less. The theme of their efforts was **"I Am A Man"**.

The marches were a march of *hope* for me. I was suffering from low self-esteem. That was instilled in me at an early age. I thought I was the ugliest child *"nappy hair and dark skin"* was not popular in my community, Orange Mound. I also had a scar on my face that came from a fall on the floor furnace when I was younger.

Members of the SCLC changed all of that for me. They shampooed my hair and gave me probably the first afro in Memphis. I had never seen an afro worn on anyone in Memphis before.

Unlike Hester, I had a father and mother in my home. My father, Ernest, was a construction worker and chauffeur and my mother, Jenny, was a homemaker. My father was very instrumental in raising my four sisters and me. Often my mother was institutionalized and was unable to care for us.

I found my refuge in *Reading*. I developed an insatiable appetite for reading and developed my own mini Library. I wasn't so much interested in boys so the adventures in my books were fascinating.

My father grew more vigilant, as I grew more involved with the Civil Rights Movement, SCLC youth choir, passing out honey buns to the striking sanitation workers and other civil activities. In my father's words **"Jail No Bail"**. But I knew the sanitation workers and the families in my neighborhood deserved more. These families were among the poorest families in our neighborhood. When I learned that Dr. Martin Luther King, Jr. was coming to Memphis, I wondered whether he was really supported by black folks. I had heard conflicting stories. Also, at that time, I was torn between Malcolm X, Stokely Carmichael, and other civil rights leaders that wanted a more direct approach to our civil rights.

I was never afraid of the violence in my community other than the violence coming from the police. However, I was introduced to fear when I heard glass breaking and folks running for their lives on March 28th, 1968, when the piece was breached at that King march. I have never witnessed that many people turn and run. It was horrifying. We subsequently assembled back at Clayborn Temple African Methodist Christian Church, where most of the protest meetings were held in the starting point for the Marches On City Hall

    When Dr. King return and spoke at Mason Temple the night of April 3rd, I sat behind him in the choir where he gave his last speech. Little did we know that this would be the last time that we would see him alive.

    The next day, my sister, Mary Hunt, the young lady in the famous picture standing on the balcony pointing in the direction from which the shot was fired, would witness the murder on the Lorraine Motel balcony. I was now scared for her especially when she was interrogated by the police. However, I was more fearful after Dr. King's death when the National Guard with guns and bayonets, lined the streets in our neighborhood. I have never seen anything like that before. It was **truly frightening.**

Despite the violence that took place, I found hope. I was led to believe we could organize and make a positive difference. I was motivated to improve myself by finishing high school and earning a college degree. I graduated from Melrose High School, Clark College (now Clark Atlanta University), and earned my law degree from Memphis State (now the University of Memphis).

I felt I could best serve my people and my community through learning and practicing law. However, the experience of that tumultuous time of 1967 to 1968 prepared me to face whatever difficulties that were in store for me in the future. It was that experience and learning that prepared me to be elected as the first African American female judge in the city of Memphis in 1990.

16N68: My Story can be the story of many young African Americans living in Memphis fighting for freedom, dignity, and equality during that time.

Thanks, my friend Hester, for sharing your story.

Judge Earnestine Hunt Dorse
Municipal Court
City of Memphis

"The fight doesn't stop as the years go by."
Hester J. Moore

PREFACE

As I approached the age of 16, I had witnessed enough footage on the Nightly News of horrific scenes of black protesters marching peacefully only to be met by the police officers garnishing hoses with water, the force and the impact of which, would knock the protesters down to their knees as they landed on the street and concrete sidewalk. Unable to get up the fallen protesters were then beaten by the police with billy clubs, as dogs lunged to tear their flesh from their bones. Terrified with my eyes open wide, I feared for the sanitation workers who were on strike here in Memphis. I prayed nightly, *"Lord, please don't let this happen in Memphis."*

Late one evening during the 1964 presidential election, I was glued to the black-

and-white TV. As this unlikely spokesperson, a stout black woman, a poor uneducated woman from Mississippi spoke before the Democratic National Convention. She recounted many times when her life was targeted with threatening phone calls day and night. Fired from her job and beaten merciless, but still determined to give Blacks in her County the vote. I watched this brave woman and have never forgotten, Fannie Lou Hamer as she stood her ground and plodded on, her image, her broken English, her strength would stay with me forever. She was 45 years old before she could vote. Fannie Lou Hamer said, *"Sometimes it seems like to tell the truth today is too run the risk of being killed. But if I fall, I'll fall 5'4" forward in a fight for freedom. Cause I ain't backing off."*

Then Medgar Evers, NAACP field secretary for the state of Mississippi and World War II veteran was gunned down in his driveway at his home. Evil men's threats became real. If you get out of line this could happen to you. His blood-soaked, lifeless body was a image for all the world to see.

Then there were three college students, James Chaney, Michael Schwerner and Andrew Goodman, they were falsely arrested and disappeared. Day after day we watch for an update of the missing three college students, then their bodies where found, they had been tortured and murdered. I and the world were devastated.

Viola Liuzzo, a young white mother who lived in Detroit, Michigan. She volunteered to come to Alabama. She told her husband *"I must go, I've got to do something."* She was gunned downed by the KKK as a reminder that a white woman should never be riding in a car with a black man. She paid the ultimate price.

Many Freedom Fighters lost their lives like the ones that I have mentioned above. However their deaths and the deaths of Dr. King and Senator Bobby Kennedy left a profound effect on me. After their deaths, was a time that I felt I turned my back on the Civil Rights Movement. I didn't want to die. I wasn't ready to die. I wasn't ready to lay my life down at 16.

I was deeply afraid for the sanitation workers and anyone that was involved in the protest. I was afraid for myself. I'd seen enough, heard enough and read enough that if you were black one should stay in his or her place or suffer the consequences. I simply did not want to die.

After accepting the request to come to Memphis, Dr. King sent word to the clergymen that he wanted more youth involved in the boycott of the downtown stores. Two teachers from my school pulled me aside and asked me if I would be interested in participating with other youth. I didn't hesitate. Strangely, without hesitation, I said yes.

I often declared the words *"let the grown people handle grown people business,"* but deep down inside I wanted to help. I just didn't know how. I didn't have a clue to our role with the adults. Dr. King insisted that before we march, we had to endure a rigorous non-violent training. Each day on the streets of Downtown Memphis, I took the fear and thoughts, and the possibility that I could be killed with me, but I couldn't turn around. After the failed march of March 28th, I was waiting for the day that we could march again. However that march never took place because Dr. King was killed on April 4th 1968.

When you engage in history-making the authority of a specific moment in time can leave a lasting impression. This time in my life left an indelible imprint. I endured years of confusion, fear, hate and guilt, that I simply didn't do enough. As I became older, I made myself invisible to the Civil Rights Movement. Back then it is unlikely that I conceived the notion of how these events affected me. How they shaped the Blackness of my Womanhood and caused me to grow and become aware of the price that Black America had faced and what they are still facing today.

In my moments of despair, which was often, I had to come to myself. I had to realize that each of us has a role to play *"In This Thing Called Life."* My role was to be walking in the hall one day when two teachers approached me. That I would accept the invitation to participate in picketing of downtown stores. To give in to a rigorous training. I could have turned my back and went home, but I didn't. My role as a 16-year-old was to be serious about a serious matter. My role as a 16-year-old was to experience what it was like to fear death. My role was to come to grip with all of those emotions of death and destruction, and say thank you God for the journey.

    I wrote *16N68: My Story* as a homage to the individuals that have crossed my path with a word of wisdom, or a pat on the shoulder: Ben and Francis Hooks, Maya Angelou, Samuel Kyles, Elaine Turner, Osupa Moon, Ossie Davis, Alvenia Fulton, Reverend Jesse Jackson, Rev. Johnson E. Saulsberry, Jr. Queen Akua, Ekpe Obioto, the Lee Family, Dr. Peola Dews, Ernest Withers, Morgan Freeman, Charles Cartwright, Professor Clarence Christian, Coach Jerry Johnson, Curtis Dillahunt, Fannie Delk, and Moms Mabley.

    My role today is to continue to tell my story. To offer a helping hand to a struggling youth. To listen to that youth with understanding. Encourage that youth. Advise that youth with love and appreciation. Appreciation of the engaging minds of our youth and supporting them in efforts to change the world. Today, I am well with the part that I played in the movement. A fraction of a bigger picture but an important one.

This book ***16N68: My Story***, is a fraction of the many ***Untold Stories*** of the civil rights movement. A movement of students, everyday citizens, educated, uneducated, preachers, union leaders, lawyers, actors, politicians, men, women, children, rallying to stand up to the evil of injustice. My experience brimmed with the range of emotions, thoughts, and uncertainty. From bold courage, to almost paralyzing fear, to unnerving edginess, and a inexplainable joy. My young warriors your books are in the making. Your experience with the rising of others is to Stamp Out oppression. Stamp Out racism. It won't be easy, but the work has to be done. Remember when you shout out ***"Black Lives Matter"*** shout it out unapologetically. Don't allow the events of 2020 to destroy your goals.

"Change will not come if we wait for some other person or some other time. We are the ones we have been waiting for. We are the change that we seek."

President Barack Obama

TABLE OF CONTENTS

SECTION ONE: EARLY DAYS

CHAPTER 1: My Friend Linda Kelly — 25
CHAPTER 2: Mama & Early Adolescence — 37
CHAPTER 3: Chasing Charles Moore — 44
CHAPTER 4: Mama Was A Radical — 51

SECTION TWO: TURNING 16

CHAPTER 5: Summer of '67 – Eleventh Grade — 73
CHAPTER 6: Fall of '67 – Eleventh Grade — 85

PHOTO PAGES

High School; Media; Storytelling — 109

SECTION THREE: THE MARCH

CHAPTER 7: The Day Everything Changed — 115
CHAPTER 8: Dr. King Comes To Memphis — 123
CHAPTER 9: The Night Before It All Went Wrong — 137
CHAPTER 10: Are We Gonna Die? — 149
CHAPTER 11: Death of Dr. Martin Luther King, Jr. — 157

CHAPTER 12: On The Steps Of City Hall	169
CHAPTER 13: Civil Rights Affect On My Life	177
CHAPTER 14: Married & Pregnant By April 1969	183
CHAPTER 15: No Prom	191
CHAPTER 16: 30 Years After – 1998	195
CONCLUSION: Importance Of Telling Our Stories	201
I THANK YOU	208
SPECIAL ACKNOWLEDGEMENT	209
AUTHOR BIO	213

16N68: My Story
Section One:
Early Days

"We should live our lives as though Christ was coming this afternoon."
Jimmy Carter

CHAPTER 1
MY FRIEND LINDA KELLY

"Do you believe I'm gonna shoot you?" Brenda Lewis teasingly asked her friend Linda. Linda was busy braiding Brenda's sister Joyce's hair as Joyce sat at Linda's feet.

"Gone girl gone witcha playing." Linda responded waving her hand to Brenda so to finish Joyce's hair. School was tomorrow and Linda had stayed much too long already at the Lewis' home.

Mr. Lewis' double barrel shotgun was kept in the far corner. He had gone hunting the day before and he kept his gun fully loaded, after a rash of peeping toms had stalked the neighborhood.

Brenda awkwardly struggled to pick up the heavy shotgun, which was propped in the corner. She reached for the trigger. She cocked the gun and put her finger on the trigger.

"I told you, I'm gonna shoot you!"

"KABOOM!!!!!" the barrage of shotgun pellets struck Linda in the chest. Her left arm nearly ripped off, she fell backward, and then slowly got up and stumbled toward the door screaming. Stunned and confused, with glazed eyes wide-open Linda collapsed and began to roll backward, and slowly sprawled out on the floor gasping for breath. Gushes of blood and body flesh splashed throughout the room and in Joyce's hair. Linda died seconds later. The screams of the other girls erupted with horror and disbelief.

Chaos and confusion consumed the room. Mr. Lewis frantically ran into the room as the terrified girls clumsily ran, falling over each other in panic. The sound of the gun was so explosive, that neighbors began to pour out of their homes to see what had happened.

My Friend

I remember Linda and I giggled like most 13 and 14-year-old girls on many days as we walked to or from school. Especially since boys were our main topic of the day. We had much to talk about during these walks. Not so much talk about anything else. Actually, other things were quite boring in comparison.

My dear friend Linda Kelly had a grown woman's figure. It was as if she wasn't aware of this appeal about herself, and often times the boys of Carver High School would hit on her, and she responded by giving a slight innocent grin while ignoring their advances.

I admired her for that. Shooing off the boys. I admired her for so many other things. She spoke in a way that was soft and sweet. I never heard her ever use cuss words, nor raise her voice.

Linda's grandparents were quite old, and they were the ones raising her. I never asked why she lived with them, but I later found out through conversations with Wilma McGee that Linda came to Memphis from

Detroit. Somehow it seemed like she just appeared in the neighborhood out of nowhere.

During the writing of this book I had many talks with Wilma McGee, another friend in the neighborhood whose father was a sanitation worker. She said, Linda's mother lived in Detroit, and Linda always desired to go back home. Linda never shared this information with me. I actually thought that she was from Mississippi. As for years, it was rumored she was from there.

Her beautiful black hair was always pressed to perfection. She even had permission to wear earrings. They were fake pearls and pierced. She could wear a little makeup and wear stockings to school. I could only wear stockings on Sundays, and they were usually my big sister's cast-offs, usually full of runs and holes in the toes. Her best look was when she wore a black fitted skirt, and a white blouse with black flats.

Sometimes we exchanged clothes, although her clothes were prettier than mine, and she had more clothes than I did. If my

Mama found out that I was exchanging clothes, I would have gotten the worse whuppin'. We had to be very slick about changing clothes without getting caught.

Lipstick panty hose, tight skirts, drop-top convertibles and double dating, staying out until 12 midnights with boys consumed our conversations. Somehow, in our minds we felt we would acquire all of these things when we turned 16.

Wow, turning 16 meant the world to us! My mother did tell me that I could start receiving boys over to the house at age 15 (I did have enough nerve to ask).

At some point, I thought Micheale had messed things up for me, with her getting pregnant at 17. It was a bummer, but Mama kept her promise anyway.

My sister Joyce got married at 15 and had a baby so she was done. Peggy was too young. My unmarried sister, Dorothy already had five children, and Ethel, my sanctified sister was waiting to go to heaven. She did want to get married but most of her guy friends that I saw walking her home were what we called "sissy" types, Larry Cunning and Jo Joseph (Jo-Jo) Bell. I knew sex was not on Ethel's mind. At least I thought so. Hollis Hill was her main squeeze but Mama did not worry about her. Ethelle (her official name today) was trying to do the right thing.

Linda was the only person in my neighborhood that I truly felt a friendship with. I dared not talk about boys to other girls in my neighborhood, such as Daisy and Dessie, two sisters from Mississippi. They were much too country. Dana, another girl, was nasty, and most of the other girls that I knew were already *"doing it."*

Talking to my sisters or Mama about boys was out of the question. That would have been taboo. Getting caught talking to a boy by one of my brothers was a sure indication that Mama would be told, so I had to be careful to play the role that I was not interesting in those *"stupid boys."*

As a little girl, in the first and second grade, my Mama thought it was cute for me to have a little boyfriend. I would gleefully come home after school and tell her who my boyfriend was for the day or week. She would smile and not say anything but give a look like *"that's so cute."* Linda and I were excited about turning sixteen in sixty-eight and graduating the next year in sixty-nine. We couldn't wait!

I sleepily looked over at the black long sleeve sweater that I had borrowed, which Linda had called about earlier, to remind me to get it over to her before her grandmother found out that I had it. She promised she would let me have it again if I brought it back before the day was over. I had such terrible acne, and this turtleneck was just the sweater to cover any unsightly bumps.

This Sunday evening started like any other lazy Sunday. However, later that evening was filled with screams of despair coming from the far end of Michigan and Olive streets.

Loud screams and folks cussing each other out was a usual occurrence so I did not bother to check it out. I thought when it was time, I would get the lowdown. I took a deep breath to gather myself to take this walk and see what the commotion was about.

Taking my time, I walked slowly, making my way through the crowd that had gathered at the Lewis' front yard. An ambulance whisked past me. Puzzled. I could not get a good look at who could have met their fate from something gone terribly wrong. Mrs. Lewis had died the day before, in my mind I assumed Mr. Lewis had a dreadful heart attack.

Then someone said *"Linda, Linda Kelly was shot and killed!"*

I whispered her name as I glanced down at her sweater. *"Dead"* I whispered *"but her sweater..."* I said to myself, *"Linda!"* I stood there confused and shaken. The thought of someone getting killed was bad enough, but *"Linda Kelly. No way! No. Not Linda!"*

People were crying and some were talking and milling around. The Mitchells were there, Charles, Constance, James, Ronald, and Patricia. The McGees also were there, Roy, Wilma, Joann, and Darnell. Wilma was supposed to have been at the Lewis' home that Sunday, but she told me later that something else had come up and she wasn't there when it happened.

In addition, more neighbors: the fat man with the good wavy hair that lived right at the corner of Michigan and Olive with his five daughters, Mrs. Campbell and her children Darryl, (whom I had crushed on but he ended being the best man in my wedding) Lucille, Wardean, Onetha. Sister Norrine Miles ("*Sister Bird Legs*" my Mama's private nickname for her) and her grandsons Ricky and Gary, the light skin and the dark skin Bell families, and Mrs. Juanita and her husband (the couple with the boxer dogs and pretty tulips) were also there.

Stunned and in disbelief, I deliberately walked back home as slowly as I could, my eyes staring at the ground. I couldn't cry. I just couldn't. I couldn't make myself cry one tear. Sorting out in my mind the horror that that **Linda** was killed. It seemed impossible to grasp that unimaginable senseless act. After all we were only 13 and 14 at that time. She was a year older, and we both were only in the eighth grade.

Nightfall was hovering over the sun and emptiness filled my soul. *"God help me. Only old people die! Lord, don't let this be true! Not my friend, not my friend Linda!'*

When I arrived home, I told Mama the bad news about Linda being killed but it didn't seem to faze her one bit. She never said *I'm sorry"* or asked me *"How was I doing? "*

The only question she asked was, *"Didn't Mrs. Lewis just pass away yesterday? And now this."* I didn't answer. I knew Mrs. Lewis, Brenda's mama, died yesterday, but I could care less. My friend was gone forever. **Forever!**

Getting ready for school, the following morning was extremely difficult for me. Linda and I always walked to school together.

The Day After Linda's Death

The next morning, I approached Linda's house. I waited for her to come out, smiling, closing the door behind her, and then we would walk to school as we always did. *"Please Linda open the door. Please open the door."*

I waited. Staring at her door. Nothing happened. Please Linda come out. Let yesterday be a dream, but it wasn't. This was real. It wasn't a dream at all. I will never forget those days when I passed by Linda's home. I could hear her grandmother weeping and calling Linda's name. I didn't have the nerve to stop. I just couldn't. *"Linda, Linda, Oh Lord, Linda. My baby!!!"*

As I entered the cafeteria, muffle voices of Linda's name could be heard but conversations weren't something I could clearly understand. The look of sadness on the faces was felt as I past tables of students talking and staring at me.

During her funeral, many classmates were fainting. Some of them were running down the aisles of the church, screaming and calling out her name. *"Linda!!!!!! Oh Why? Oh! Why God???? Why???"* I forced myself to make my way to the casket. There she laid, my dear precious friend, **Linda**. She was beautiful laying there as she publicly slept forever. Not one tear left my eyes. Then I turned away and saw so many weeping with grief and loss. Her grandmother was so overcome with grief that I don't believe she was even there. It was too much, way too much! I exited the church to get some fresh air. I stared at her name on the hearse, and spelled her name aloud:

"L.I.N.D.A. K.E.L.L.Y."

This is my friend's name on this hearse. After this, she will be buried. She is **Dead**. She is going in the ground. I had never had a friend die. I wanted Linda to come back. Now she was gone and she would never come back. **Never!** I smoothed my hand over her engraved name and looked at all the kids and grown-ups around me, but I couldn't shed a tear. I was numb as I waited for my Mama to pick me up. When she did, I didn't say a word. I just stared out the window. I couldn't cry. **Not one tear.**

"If there is no struggle, there is no progress."
Frederick Douglass

CHAPTER 2
MAMA & MY EARLY ADOLESCENCE

I had my share of men poking at me too. It started around the age of 10.

This disfigured arm older thug, Lefty, a loud rambunctious character, brother to Ugly Baby and Eugly baby (the twins), called me over one day and grabbed me in my private area. I was shocked and could not believe that he would do such a thing. I backed off and sternly looked him in the face, but I couldn't speak. I did not say a word. The other drunks that were hanging around said *"Mane you wrong for that. That Ollie Kirk sister."* It seem not to bother him, he cussed and walked off. I never told my brother, Ollie Kirk because I never wanted trouble. This was my brother's hangout and either my brother would get hurt or Lefty would. I did not want to take a chance.

There was an upstanding mother of a church. My mother had to visit to her to fix her hair. She weighed every bit of 600 pounds. I never saw her leave her home but she did walk around in the house, but I do not think that she could walk down the steps of her home to leave. My mother's brother once stay with Sister Ramsey.

We would come to watch television with Sister Ramsey, but she looked at the news all the time so we did not visit her much. One day Mr. Jeff, another neighbor, was visiting her at the same time as my siblings and I were there. She called us over as if to show Mr. Jeff something. We all surrounded her and one by one she fondled us by putting her hands in our panties and searching around as if she was looking for money but she only gave us a penny. We did not know then that she was molesting us.

My sister's boyfriend would stare at me and pull me up to him; bragging what a fine chick I will be when I got older. The look on my sister's face told me that I needed to go in the house and I did.

As a child, I would spend hours in front of the mirror talking to myself. I was waiting for Troy Donahue (Google him) to come kiss me and take me away. I made up characters of villains, damsels in distress and leading women. I was mesmerized with being swept away never to live in Memphis again – ever!

I guess I should explain, at eleven, something drastic happened. Micheale, my next in line above me sister, had to take me to the neighborhood clinic. She returned home with me in tow telling mama, **"Hester weighs 100 pounds!"** Hester weighs 100 pounds at eleven years old! I was looking at Michaele like *"What was the fuss?"* Then soon after that the neighborhood kids, brothers, and sisters began to call me *"fat hog"*. Once when I was older, my brother Jerry introduced me as *"his fat sister, Hester."* As if, he had to apologize for me being overweight

I remember eating day old jelly and chocolate donuts every day. The jelly and icing oozing on my tongue; ready for me to lick the dripping before it hit the ground. I would stand in front of Weona store; my eyes closed in bakery heaven. *"Umm! This is some good stuff."* Margaret Boykins, a neighborhood bully burst my bubble one day when she stood there witnessing my heavenly bliss while I was eating a donut *"You so fat. Look at you eating all those sweets."* I did not know why she was standing there with her face, scrunched up minding my business so I ran home.

It did not help that the older women in the neighborhood would point out to me *"Ooo girl you gonna be just like your mama, you gone be made up just like her."* My mother had this very small waistline, bigger than big butt and these humongous legs. I had no idea that she was fine as wine. I saw her as a big fat woman that when she walked her butt looked like Jell-O shaking, moving to the beat of a slow song. Hence, I went through years of fighting that fat demon.

When I would have to go places with her, I tried to slightly walk behind her. I felt somewhat ashamed that she was not skinny like some of my friend's mothers. I dragged behind her just a little bit; watching her massive body and long strides with her purse clinging to her side. She usually started out holding my hand as we left Michigan Street but somehow I always slipped my hand away from her. I was looking to see who was looking at her. Her presence was commanding.

She was this high yella woman with green eyes, sandy hair, almost six feet tall, wore a 12-size shoe and her hands were big as a man. She had already told us many stories of having to defend herself. On one occasion two men tried to get her drunk to rape her but she outsmarted them and was able to get away. She also told us how she use to hop trains from Mississippi to Memphis.

"*Hi Mrs. Johnson*" neighbors would speak. She would speak back in her southern drawl *"Hey hawney or haay babee"*. One by one, the men from across the street and way way across the street would speak to her. Mr. Tidmore, Miss Bunch's husband who had a speech impediment lived in the back of us would say, *"Umm Umm Mrs. Dohnson you sho got some big o purdy legs."* His wife would respond *"Hush up ole fool and leave hur alone".* Mr. Tidmore would then turn to his wife and had the nerve to asked could he feel my Mama's legs with wive's permission. Miss Bunch would then ask my Mama *"Can this fool feel the back of yo legs Mrs. Johnson."* My Mama would paused and then say yes. *"Ok. If you say he can."* Mr. Tidmore would put his hands around my mother's calf and yell out *"OOOOweee Lord ham murcy Mrs. Dohnson you sho gotsome big o purdy legs!"* Everyone around would yelp with laughter because it was a funny sight, but at the same time, it made me uncomfortable and embarrassed.

    I didn't really have anyone I could talk to about things that bothered me so I just kept it bottled up inside. We never told our mother any of the stuff that happened to us, like the time when the deformed arm guy, Lefty touched me or Sister Ramsey fondling us. We couldn't. We lived with the fear that if we told it somebody was going get killed or she would kill us. Either way, it was a risk that we didn't want to take. She was the only parent we had.

Mama was a strict disciplinarian and carried a .22 pistol that spoke volumes. Even years later at 16, we could not leave the porch without permission. We really could not do much of anything without her permission. We could do nothing at all. And if we did, we suffered. Our asses were gravy. We stood or sat on our high raised porch most of the time, passing the time away, either braiding each others hair, playing with a stick doll or boy watching.

If I have painted a picture of a mad woman, you make that choice. On the other side of that, we also felt that if we told her about someone messing with us, that she might kill them and go to jail. We lived with these opposing fears *"fear of her and fear of losing her."* We loved our mother.

"Hold fast to dreams, for if dreams die, life is a broken-winged bird that cannot fly. Hold fast to dreams."
   Langston Hughes

CHAPTER 3
CHASING CHARLES MOORE

Another thing my Mama did not know about her sweet little girl was I had been chasing Charles, an older boy, ever since I was in the eighth grade. He was in the twelfth grade. Actually I began conjuring up how I would meet him the summer I passed to the seventh grade.

When I heard him interviewed on the radio station WDIA, I knew that I had to meet Charles. There was something about his voice that drew me. For some reason, I needed to know him. Matter of fact, I even felt like God wanted me to meet him. Even then I had the thought that God wanted me to marry him.

Crazy huh! He had been injured at football practice and ended up losing his leg due to an infection. I never knew anyone with one leg. When I got to Carver, I didn't know that he was being homeschool. I looked for him for the entire fall semester.

    The next spring, during school one day, in the eighth grade, I had walked over to the B building from the A building. As I was about to make a right to go to Mr. McClellan's spelling class, I heard Miss Weed, one of the English teachers say, *"Young man ... Charles Mo, where you going?"* I froze and turned around. It's him, this guy has to be him. He turned to Miss Weed and said, *"Class"*. She responded, *"Well Charles Mo you better not be late."*

    I looked at him in amazement. He was fine. Oh! My goodness. He had this rust orange color sweater and matching pants and that limp gave him a swagger and groove. When he talked and opened his mouth, the gap in the middle of his teeth was right on time. Then there were his Japanese shaped eyes. Oh my goodness he was so handsome! I thought I was going to faint. I just saw him for the first time and I wanted to be his girlfriend!

Somehow I found out on the last period of school each day he and one of his best friends, John Rankin, would walk over from the A building to the B building breezeway as they were leaving school. I encouraged one of my friends, Marie Bratcher to skip class so we could be standing there in that very spot where John Rankin and Charles Moore would pass. The first time this operation happened, Charles and John passed by as we expected, so my friend and I pretended that we were talking to each other. I was emotionally overcome and it was too much for me to bear, so I turned my back and Marie did all the talking. John and Charles spoke back. My heart pounded like a running fool. She spoke. They spoke. I could have died. *"Oh my God, Charles Moore spoke to us."* He didn't even really see me. He spoke to my back. This went off and on for a whole semester of us placing ourselves in the right spot when he and John would leave school.

One day John Rankin said something very unexpected, *"Charles you are going to marry that funny looking girl"*. I almost died. Sometimes I could catch him and Edward Gaskin, another friend of his, walking together or he would walk with this crazy guy Mitch. It didn't make any difference to me who else was there as long as I could get a glimpse of this Charles Moore.

Then the big thing happened. Marie and I skipped class to go to the pep rally designated for the 9-12th grade. After scanning the gym where the pep rally was to take place, she spotted Charles sitting with Lonnie Lowe (another hunk) one of Charles' running buddies. Ida Ballard, a majorette and popular girl sat in front of them. We bravely walked over and place ourselves close by. I was so nervous. I told Marie to ask Charles for his number. He agreed to give it to her but no one had a pen or pencil. He agreed to still give it to her if we could locate a pencil before we left. I kept my eye on him because I did not want him to get a way. After the pep rally, I lagged behind him, he didn't appear like he was trying to get a pencil at all so when we passed Mr. Hunt's room I ask Mr. Hunt for a pencil. Charles wrote his number down. It looked like chicken scratch but who cared. I did not. I handed the pencil back to Mr. George Hunt. Hunt made a comment to Charles, *"You at it again"*. Charles just smiled. When Charles walked off, I could have peed in my panties. *"We have his number! We have his number! Oh my God!"* I told Marie to keep number because I did not want to lose it.

My phone rang the following Sunday. It was Marie. She was so excited that she could barely speak. I asked her what was wrong. She kept repeating, *"You go with him! "You go with him!"* I remembered asking her to calm down and tell me why was she so excited? *"Ok,"* she said taking a deep breath. *"I called Charles and asked him would he go with me and he said Yesssss!"* I said to her *"What?"* Marie said, *"He said yes! But, I told him that my name is Hester Johnson and that I met him at the pep rally."* I was stunned. I was speechless. *"Are you sure that he said that he would go with Me.?"* I gasped. ***"Yes!"*** Marie said it again. *"He said* *that he would go with you!!!!"* I could hardly contain myself. I remember thinking. I'm only 13 and how am I going to date this boy? He is in the 12th grade. I couldn't act too overjoyed because I was at home. Then Marie said, *"Oh I also told him that I, you, was in the 10th grade!"*

"Ok. Ok. I'm in the 10th grade and what else did he say?" I demanded. Marie replied, *"Nothing"*. I just asked, *"Whether he would go with me and he said yessss! Now all you have to do is call him back as if it was you talking to him,"* she said. *"What would I say?"* I responded. *"I don't know, but he did say that he would go with you."* I took a deep breath and I called him. *"He answered. He answered!"*

Me: *Hello, "my name is Hester Johnson."*
Charles: *"Yes, didn't I just get through talking to you?"*
Me: *"Yes"*
Me: *"Whatcha doing?"*
Charles: *"Nothing. Talking to you."*
Me: *"Oh yeah you is."*
Me: *"You gonna go with me?"*
Charles: *"Yes, I told you I would, didn't I."*
Me: *"Thanks. Ok, bye."*

Charles: *"Bye."*

After formally introducing myself to him face to face, I began to see him more at school. It took some shuffling for me hiding my spelling and arithmetic books. After all, if I was in the 10th grade, I would not be hauling those eighth grade books around. I felt so special when he would walk me from Study Hall. Ninth through 12th grade would dismiss at 2:15 and the 7th and 8th graders would dismiss at 3:30, so I had to lie and tell him that I had to wait and pick up my little sister after school. I did have a little sister, Peggy in the 7th grade but she knew her way home and she never had to wait on me.

This was hard because even when I would come out of study hall, which was his last period, I had spelling to go to. I was always late and had to see Mr. Lloyd Stovall (Sugarfoot) the assistant principal. But I was in love and I didn't care what I had to do to see Charles Moore.

'There comes a time when people get tired of being plunged into the abyss of exploitation and nagging injustice."
Dr. Martin L. King, Jr.

CHAPTER 4
MAMA WAS A RADICAL

It was very important for me to let you know who I was before 1968. I was a silly, timid girl who wanted to be loved and I experienced many of the things other kids my age experienced. Playing in the neighborhood with my sisters, doing what Mama told us, being bullied or called hurtful names, chasing boys and dreaming of being grown -- for me 16 was the magic number.

I do remember having a deep heart feeling for the underdog. Hell, I didn't know that I was an underdog too. We lived in a three room duplex, plastic posted on holes in the walls, roaches, rats and many times sleeping in the dark. My father wasn't around and I just wanted to be loved or to fit in. I wanted to look like everybody else. I didn't want to be different.

My mother was a radical in her own right and maybe I was more like her than I wanted to be. We could not understand why she was so ornery. Her children thought she was. We knew that she was very protective of us that she had a fight in her -- like me.

She used that aggression at church often times when the Pastor would ask the congregation to look over the person next to you and say, *"I'm blessed"*. She refused. Mama always did the opposite of what the pastor would say as if to get his attention that he could not tell her what to do. The motherboard asked all the mothers of the church to wear white and Mama wore black. She dared anyone to say anything to her and they did not. They did not have the nerve. She later told us when she was around 80 years old that *"All my life folks been telling me what to do and now I ain't going to do nothing 'les I want to."* End of story. Mama always bragged on being the first woman to ever be called *Mrs.* in the newspaper. For years women were referred to in the Memphis Press-Scimiter newspaper by their first names. Blacks were threatening to boycott the evening paper for not referring to grown Black women as Mrs. I guess in all of us Black folks, somewhere there was a fight in us, even the most docile individual.

We stayed in our own area or neighborhood and mostly did not venture to far away because folks from other neighborhoods did not take kindly to outsiders. Everybody pretty much knew each other in our neighborhood.

Seemed as if everybody surely knew my Mama, Lorsey is what most neighbors call her. If I did, anything on Trigg and one of the neighbors witnessed it like Mrs. Bertie Mae or the Robinsons, my Mama would find out. If I did anything on Olive Street, there the Whites (kin to the Grices) Mama would know it, and forget about Michigan Street, Ms. Betty, Ms. Pudding and her husband Mr. Ray or Mrs. Hawkins would tell about anything I got into and my butt was dead meat. From Michigan, Trigg, Olive and Florida Streets, everybody knew Mrs. Johnson and all those children, whether they were all hers or my nieces and nephews or someone that mother had taken in.

So we could not understand why late one night this light skin boy walked up to my mother and as he passed her, he attempted to snatch her purse. We were waiting for her to come home but we were caught up watching Tarzan this late Saturday night. We did not hear the commotion. The boy yelled at my mother to let go of her purse but she held on. An elderly man had passed by, but later he said to the police that he thought she was tousling with a child of hers. As the robber jerked on the purse, he kicked her in the process but she fought back and grabbed him and held on. He finally got away from her and ran off. Somehow my Mama scared that boy so bad or wrestled so hard that he dropped his wallet and the other stuff he had. Mama grabbed it all up. As she gathered herself, she rushed in the house to tell us what happened.

When the police came and took her to the hospital, she was met with the doctors teasing her, *"Look there is the lady that robbed the robber. She took his wallet while he was trying to steal hers."* They had a big laugh but we often wondered who this person could have been because my mother did not take any mess from anyone. He should have known that.

Mama said *"He wasn't gonna take her hair dressing money."* They later caught the young man with the identification he dropped. Our neighborhood had it share winos, thugs, dice playing, and pool playing Negroes like any other neighborhood. However, we had other folks that were getting their diplomas, going to college, and owning businesses. Upright folks like the Johnsons, Grices, Lanes, McGees, Bakers, Robinson, Flemings, Robinsons and the Fords.

The Bakers and the Gowdys ran a sundry store from their homes. Often time if Mr. Gowdy stood on his porch waiting for us to shop with him, he knew right away that we were going up to the Weona store. Mr. Sam and Ms. Beverly owned this store or we would shop with Mr. Albert. Mr. Albert was white. He had white blonde hair, stark blue eyes and white hair on his arms. He was a bit mean so we didn't shop there much.

Mr. Gowdy would begin ranting about us passing his store to shop further down. We would pretend as if we did not hear him. He would get vicious like. *"They don't care about yawl, they gone take your money and spend it in their own neighborhoods."* We would not look over because we had to go to the store Mama sent us to. He sounded like a preacher preaching, ranting and shouting. *"Do not support those white folks. They do not care about yawl"*. Mr. Sam of Weona had what Mr. Gowdy didn't have. **"Credit."** If you were in good standing, you could get your groceries on credit at Weona. He also offered delivery in a station wagon and he gave young boys jobs. Mr. Sam had hog jawls, neckbones, sugar, rice, corn meal; all the necessities Black folks needed each week. Weona was a cramped supermarket but a business that worked with the neighbors. He had shopping carts and aisles; you actually felt like you were in a big grocery store. Then he offered butchers to cut up your meat. Britt Lee, one of the Grice's daughters husband was the main butcher. You look over the meat you wanted then he weigh it and gave you a price. He also gave me bones for my dogs. What he didn't know, some of those bones were good bones so before the dogs chewed on them, Mama would use them for soup.

Some days we would go into Mr. Grumpy and Mrs. Gowdy's store and stand at the display case of goodies and point to what we wanted. Or you could get ice cream, drinks or cigarettes. He had other things but his selection was limited.

We rarely shopped with the Bakers. First of all, their home was at the very edge to a winding downhill road. The house sat on the left in front of the Fords. It was dark down there and they were mostly closed. Mrs. Baker was very snooty and talked country proper, so we did not fool with her much. The children, Laura, John, Joseph, Mary and Gerald mostly worked the Sundry. The stuff there was little of nothing so we didn't waste time going. Nevertheless, these Black folks were business owners right there in our neighborhood.

Another store was owned by Mr. Albert, the really really White man was on you when you shop at his store. If you were caught stealing in his store, he would run you down like white on rice no matter what the price of the item was. He ran after my nephew, Cecil all the way home after Cecil stole a Popsicle. Mr. Albert was not having it. He threatened to call the police on Cecil, but my sister paid for the item and Cecil was barred never again to come in his store. That might be one of the reasons his store burned down to the ground during the riots of 1968. I guess the thugs were getting back at his mean ass. When the thugs went in his store they shouted *"Ain't nothin' left here worth takin'."*

My mother fixed hair in our kitchen. I know she did not have a beauty license but she was very good at what she did and you always got good advice even if you did not asked for it. She charged two dollars and a half for regular length hair and three dollars and a quarter if you had long hair. Women would line up to be next in line. If you washed your own hair, she would give you a discount. If the line was too long, the ladies would let mama know their place in line and when it was their turn, she would send us to down to get the next lady. Her regular customers where Miss Green, All the Grices, Miss Lady, and Mrs. Mrytle. I don't know why, but Mama would walk down to Miss Robinson's each week to do her hair.

We lived in a neighborhood where nicknames were like real names and folks answered to them like the parents gave them those names. I never knew most of them by their given names. Names like Cave Man, Frog, Road Island Red, Too Pluke, Lil Snake, Big Snake, Pig Feet, Banana Nose, Ugly Baby and Eugly Baby (twins) Pop, High Boodie, Ajax, Bjax, Preacher, Omane, Black Vette, and Sugarfoot.

We had some colorful characters in our neighborhood too. Miss Nig was one of them; a very tall, dark and skinny woman. She often sat on her porch right across the street from us. Watching her was our entertainment to say the least. She was every bit of 6 feet tall, with a mouth full of snuff, her knees turned toward each other when she walked, her butt stuck up to the right as she took each step reminding you of Olive Oil on the Popeye cartoon. And when it was hot, she would clap her legs together to fan them, chewing tobacco, flapping those legs waving a piece of paper toward her skinny legs was a sight to see. *"There it goes!"* She spitted as far as she could in the street in front of her house. Big splats of big brown goo would spatter in the streets. It was nasty but as kids we thought it was hilarious. We would all laugh in our shoulders; we would not dare laugh out loud and be able to get away with it. It sure was funny.

Another memorable character was Miss I. Russell. **"OOOwee, she was a curser."** On some Saturday nights when we knew she would be fighting with her husband John, we would find a way to pass by her house to see her cut up. Miss I. Russell was a snagger-toothed, tall, big bug eyed and heavy drinker. John, her husband also drank and boy oh boy did they fight. She had this real big butt and the only two teeth that she had left in her mouth were bucked as if she sucked her thumbs at the same time. We never heard any kind of cussing like that at home. Mama used *"shit"* and *"damn"* on occasions but Miss I. Russell threatened her husband Mr. John with some awful words that we dared not repeat.

Mama had 15 children, 9 was living when I was born 3 more from my sister was born by the time I was here and we all lived in the same house. We did not have much to do. We often watched TV on another neighbor's front porch. My big sister Joyce, finally bought a black white set for us. She was tired of us sitting on neighbors front porches watching TV through the screen doors. She thought that was humiliating. There were so many of us so she bought us one.

The neighborhood boys used our backyard to play basketball. Someone put up a makeshift goal. It was just a fruit basket on an utility pole and boys would come from all over to play. It was dusty, smelly and girls were not allowed to hang out there. You could look as you walked by but you had to keep walking as not to get disrespected. All was well, no disturbance or fights until my nephew Trainer and Tweety exchanged licks because either one of them fouled way to hard. After a few blows were exchanged, others trying to stop the fight, Tweety exited out threatening to go home to get a gun. Whoa, we had never had anyone to threatened anything like this before so someone ran and told my oldest sister, Ethel. Ethel is my sanctified sister and when she began to preach and declare the word over these sinners. They soon went away. It seemed like she preached until nightfall but at least no one was shot. Tweety never came back and all was well until the next day.

We had dirt yards, black dirt yard. Sketches of green grass grew in patches throughout the yard. Garbage in barrels, boxes or leaking sacks lined along fences separating the property of Mr. and Mrs. Van Ford house way out in the back near the back of Yazoo alley. Often times, Mama would have us to sweep the backyards for paper and debris. We had it looking real pretty and clean. It didn't last long. When it rained, mud filled the barrels or anything we could put garbage in. Mud and water would fill up quickly. Running, slimy mud would pour out of the holes at the bottom of the barrels. When the men would hike the tub or barrel up to their shoulders, the grime and soot would run down the neck and back of the garbage men. One man told me later that after years of doing this he suffered awful, painful back problems.

On certain days when Mama would allow us to play in the backyard, this big ole black ashy garbage man with yellow red eyes would entertain us. We would look for him. The kids would do this same scenario each week as we got a big kick out of it. When we spotted him, someone would yell, **"There he is!"** Standing there, was this long, tall, and real black scary man. We would stand there scared to death and then plop!!! He would push his teeth; his false teeth forward, let out this hearty laugh, and say Booo! We scattered like roaches in a lighted kitchen.

Red eyes yellow eyes
*   Black blue skin*
Dirty fingernails
*   Big lips*
Stained teeth
*   Push those false teeth out*
Run!
Run!
Run!
*   We would scream, run and next week, we would do it all over again.*
Black dirt
Kicked up black dirt
Dusty black dirt
Whirled up when the wind blew
A dust storm
Run!!!!

We would run and the chickens would shriek and squawk flapping their wings.

Little chicken feet half hitting the ground, flying like.
    We respected our neighbors, we thought we knew each other business and we looked out for one another. We did not have much of

anything to do for fun. Mama would let us walk around the corner of Michigan to Trigg, Trigg to Horace Street, Olive Street back to Michigan Street. Then home. Anything we needed to do before we made it home was done. Otherwise we would have to wait until the next time. Some days, we would have asked whether we could take another loop but we did not want to bring up any suspicions of boy watching so we just settled for one trip. This was our fun.

My older brother had been stationed in California during his military service and ended up staying in Pasadena. He eventually found our daddy living with his sister our aunt, so every summer Mama would send a one or two of us kids out to see them. During the summer before 9th grade Mama decided me and my sister Ethel would go. A part of me didn't really want to go because of my crush on Charles but the girl who spent hours talking in front of the mirror, dreaming of kisses with movie stars wanted to see something outside of Memphis.

My sister Ethel and I left for Los Angeles, California. The three-day ride on the bus was horrendous. While my sister, Ethel, slept on the bus, I kissed a white boy! My lips actually touched a white boys lips! After we arrived, I ended up giving one of the biggest parties in LA at the age of 14 and staying going to Foshay Middle School in Los Angeles on Exposition. We came back to Memphis the next summer when I was turning 15. Later I learned rumors were that I was pregnant. Eew! No way Jose!

I returned to Memphis, Carver High School to attend 10th Grade. I was wigged out over the fine boys that I never knew exist, Plentimore Hobbs, Melvin Cox, Clemon Epps, Larry Dodson, Larry Morris, Jasper Miller, the list goes on. My sister Michaele gives birth to a baby girl, Angela, wow she is beautiful!

As groups of sisters and brothers, nieces and nephews, we usually headed to the store, playing *"kick the can"* if it wasn't too hot, or playing *"hide go seek"* or *"dodge ball"*. But if the ball fell in Miss Hawkins yard, that was bye bye ball. No more, ball. Miss Hawkins was a mean old soul. She was so mean that when her grandson would come over, she would let him play in her yard so we would see him. There he would be, playing with one of our balls that we had kicked in her yard. We finally started played dodge ball when she was not home. If the balls accidentally roll into her yard, we could get our bad brother Michael to get it.

I am from South Memphis, Tennessee. Born and raised. South Memphis was not a city but a place south in Memphis and where I was raised. Mostly folks went to Carver High School at 1500 Pennsylvania. Our school was named after George Washington Carver, for the famous scientist which I did not know that at the time.

I am the 14th of 15 children, I thought of myself as this pitiful, squeamish, scared, giddy girl who shied away from any **trouble**. I was never in a fight, never bullied anyone and stayed away from trouble. I surely would be the last one taking chances like boycotting downtown stores.. No way. But somehow I found myself there just a short time later. That would be trouble for sure. I was deathly scared of Mama. Boy I was I scared of gettin' whuppins! I would do all I could to get out of a them; from begging to doing work to running my Mama's bath water. At some point it began to look like an entertainment scene when it was my time to get a whuppin'. When I was about to get a whuppin', the other siblings would gather and laugh up a storm to witness it. I was begging for my life. I could see that I could get my mother to laugh at my antics so I always amped it up a notch. *"Please, please, I begged, I'll wash your hair, I'll dance for you but please do not whip me."* Sometimes it would work and some days not all the crying, begging, and snot slinging in the world worked.

  Some saw me as special. *Special?* Was I special because of my hair? Crap. I had good hair, long and coal black hair; by now, you know how our people can be if your hair texture is close to white hair, you have good hair. No one with coarse, nappy hair was getting the complements I was. Folks were telling me how pretty I was. I could not see it but strangers would come up to my mom and say, *"She sho is pretty"* My Mama would blast back and say, *"She ain't no prettier than the rest of my children."* I wouldn't say a thing. I dare not say any thing, especially since a grown-up made the statement.

A thing that you learn as a Black child growing up was the no-nos of a child's place.

You didn't interrupt two grown people talking.

You did not ask questions when given a chore.

We never asked mama what she was cooking.

We did not give our opinion on anything.

You never acted like you were mad.
You did not roll your eyes.
You did not sit between men laps.
You did not ask for money.
It was yes mam and no mam.

If you were sitting around grown folks and they were talking; you dare not repeat anything that was said that you heard. You pretended that you weren't listen when you were.

You never call a grown person a lier.

You did not interrupt your mother when she was on the phone unless it was an emergency. And it better be an emergency.

When you passed a neighbor's home, you had better speak or the neighbor would call and tell on you.

Don't look at the ground when someone talks to you especially when White people talked to you.

Do not lie. Please do not lie.

Do not steal. Please do not steal.

Lastly do not act a fool in school. Please do not act a fool in school.

16N68: MY STORY
SECTION TWO:
TURNING 16

"We all require and want respect, man or woman, black or white. It is our basic human right."
                                Aretha Franklin

CHAPTER 5
SUMMER OF 1967 – ELEVENTH GRADE

The kids in the neighborhood mostly went to George Washington Carver High School named after the inventor. Nothing was ever said about him, you didn't see any pictures hanging in the hallways to honor him but we did have a picture of the first President George Washington.

As students we were very proud of the Red and White. The Cobras had a good football and basketball team. Our principal, R.B. Thompson was daddy to most of us. My sisters and brothers attended there so I was proud to follow their examples.

On June 25 1967, I turned 16. Excited, I poised myself to soak up being 16. Wow, I am

16. This is it. My family never celebrated parties when a birthday came around. My Mama seemed to get irritated if we said anything about birthdays. *"Mama, today is my birthday."* I'd say. *"So what? You ain't the first person that celebrated a birthday and you ain't the last. Don't make a big deal out of a birthday. Just be glad that you are alive."*

We received this speech each year. But we still reminded her. I vowed that I would be different when it came to my children. I never had a birthday party as a kid. Matter of fact, I never owned a real doll for that matter. I vowed if I ever had children that they would have plenty of parties. Passing to an additional grade. Celebration. New job. Celebration. Good grades. Celebration. I ran out of giving celebrations but all my kids seemed to enjoy them.

Our celebration back then, came in the form of my siblings hitting the number of your age. Sometimes wishing that the sibling would forget that day or have mercy on you. No chance. Somebody is going to remember and look forward to a mini-beating.

However, inwardly turning 16 was a milestone for me. I could feel that my body was doing something different. I was trembling on the inside. I closed my eyes. I opened my eyes. I was engaging in thought but could not pinpoint exactly what was on my mind. Then the floodgates of tears opened. The tears started that morning and I could not stop the flood of tears. For days on end, I cried. I cried for my dear friend Linda Kelly. We were so looking forward to this day in our lives turning sixteen and she was gone. She was not here to share this time with me.

The day of braiding hair on a lazy Sunday afternoon three years ago turned out to be the death of my dear friend, Linda Kelly. We talked and shared so much and I felt so guilty that she was not here to share being sixteen with me.

Even with the sadness, I looked forward with anticipation. At the time, I could truly say that my eleventh grade year as a junior was looking good for me. Or so I thought.

School was out. The summer of 1967 was about to begin. My tenth grade year was over and June 25, 1967 would be arriving soon; the big day for me. 16 years old!!!! The 1967 graduating class of cuties, Plentimore Hobbs. Melvin Cox, Clemon Epps, Robert Hammond, Jasper Miller were all gone, so we had the whole summer to fantasize and drool over the graduating class of 1968 Robert Wooten and Steven Hayes were on the top of the list. You would have thought those boys were rock stars. Deljuan Calvin, Larry Dodson, and Harold Scott were in a singing group, *The Temprees*.

    This Summer of '67, after visiting LA for the umpteen time, my Mama came back with this silly notion that she wanted me to become "hippified". To my understanding and from witnessing the scene on television, being a hippie was meant for white people. I saw very few if any brothers and sisters participating in this nonsense. Her crazy request were for me taking my shoes off and going around barefoot, I mean in public. She brought back this oversize Afrocentric garment that she wanted me to wear. Mama gives orders, you don't asked questions, you just do what she says to do and I did what she said.

She also insisted that I wear micro minis (and asked that I report to her, if a neighbor said anything to me). She never had to be concern about how I dressed. After all my dressing would always be to her liking or if I had to wear something that churchy, I always changed once I got to school.

"*You want me to walk to the store with no shoes,*" I said. "*Yes,*" she said. "*Yes Mama,*" I responded. She was raving about the hippies and freedom of dress that she saw in Los Angeles. I'm thinking to myself *"White People"* I don't remember asking was Black folks dressing like this? When a neighbor saw me in the store, she looked puzzled and first asked, *"Where is your shoes?."* I answered her with *"Home"* then the neighbor boldly put her hand under my Dashiki, and said *"You ain't pregnant, are you?"* I said to myself, *"What? Ah Lord."* This time I am going to tell my Mama on Candy Jackson's mama, cause she really crossed the line and I did tell Mama. I don't know exactly what went down, but the two of them had a discussion about her putting her hands on me. She never did that again.

The summer of 67 was winding down and still blazing hot, my sisters and I were walking to the store, we observed this unusual young man walking toward us on Trigg Street. He was fully dressed in a loud blue suit. If you know anything about us (Black folks), and dark skin 1967; you never wore loud colors of blue, red, yellow or green clothing. If you did, that would surely signify that you were from the country, places like Mississippi, Arkansas or Alabama.

This boy was shining, blue black, tall, knock knees, bad feet (he walked funny) and his suit was about two sizes too large. He was singing to the top of lungs as if he was in a world of his own. *"Is he crazy?"* someone asked? I thought, *"This boy sounds good."* He was belting out a B.B. King song, then in the middle of that song, he flipped to Solomon Burke. He could do that instantly. His name was Isaac Simpson. In this heavy drawl, he introduced himself. *"Call me Ike."* and *"Whose you. You sho is a puurdy thang."* I replied,

"Hester, my name is Hester Johnson." He then said, *"I moved here from MissIPPI and you look like a gal that a mane can smooth up too. Gurl yous fine!"*

I wanted to laugh because he sounded so country but I wouldn't and he could sing. I didn't want to scare him off. He was a little scary himself. I wasn't interested in this boy but I did like his singing voice. My mother had already schooled me on dark skinned boys. They were not to be trusted and this one was dark skinned and some more. His teeth were sparkling white and he had these huge oversize lips. I imagined that his lips would overtake my whole head if he kissed me. That was not going to happen anyway. But it was flattering to have him tripped over his two feet for me and he always wanted to sing.

My sister Michaele was actually infatuated with Ike and she took a real liking to him. However, when he would come around; which seem like every day, he was not having it. He once told me that he didn't know that Michaele had taken a liking to him but said to me. *"Gurl you look like you dropped from heavan."*

He was good to talk to but our friendship was short lived after I asked him to take me over to this boy's house. I just wanted to say hello. At least that was my reason for wanting to go. I explained to Ike that the young man was in no way my boyfriend but someone that I had not seen in a while.

He reluctantly gave me a ride to 231 Kirk Street. I needed security to be in the car with a boy, so Michaele, my sister rode along. When we arrived at this boy's home, I slowly walked up, knocked on the door and he answered the door, shirtless. I spoke. He spoke. We talked about 3 minutes and then he said, *"No Kiss?"* I knew Ike was looking to see my reaction but if I could slightly ease behind the door, give this friend a kiss; I would be on my way. No one would be the wiser.

That is what the two of us did, we eased behind the door, we kissed. We kissed and we kissed some more. *"I have to leave."* I said. He reluctantly let me go. I left. I wasn't there 15 minutes' tops.

As I slid into the car, my sister had this strange look on her face but neither she nor Ike said a word. We all rode home in silence. I thanked Ike for taking me over and that I felt better to tell my friend hello. Michaele and I exited the car but before I exit, I gave Ike a slight kiss on the cheek. He didn't smile nor say much, so I just said I'll talk to you later.

He would probably come by tomorrow anyway with a song. We would talk, laugh and probably asked me to be his *"gurl"* and I would say no. This had gotten to be routine.

"Whew, that was over. The thrill was gone that I had for Charles." I said to Michaele. As we were climbing the stairs to the house, Michaele looked at me said, *"We saw you."* "Huh?" I said. *"We saw you. Ike and I saw you and Charles Moore kissing,"* she exclaimed. I said *"There is no way. Please tell me that you did not see me kiss Charles Moore!"*

"Yes, we saw you! You were kissing behind the door and there was a huge mirror on the opposite sidewall. We saw your reflection of the whole thing! "I told you that I liked Ike and I feel

so bad for him. You should have seen the look on his face when he saw the two of you kissing."

I was floored. I couldn't believe it. I never wanted to hurt Ike. How could I explain this to him? I didn't have to because Ike never came around again that summer.

I LOVED MUSIC AND DANCING

Late summer of 67, I had made a decision to show up unannounced at WLOK radio station. WLOK had a program of welcoming eleventh graders to audition or most were recommended to become Teen DJs for their perspective school. I really desired to be a DJ. After all someone told me that I should try but not to get too excited because, it was a close-knit group. I went every Saturday morning and sat in the lobby. I asked the right questions on how could I become a student DJ and every Saturday; I was told the same thing *"This was not the Saturday and to come back, because the former DJ's had not had their first meeting, and the period of voting had not started yet and I would have to come back."*

I did come back and I was selected to represent George Washington Carver High School. I thought Hazel Scott was a shoe in. She was either a DJ before or just popular as hell. Either way, I never saw her that summer but I didn't care, I was in. This was major for me. This would give me an opportunity to show my vocal skills off and it also made me popular with the student body especially on Fridays when getting requests to put their names on the radio was big deal. We did all the in school sport scores along with the highlights. We gave announcements and also mentioned who was dating who and my radio handle was "Handlin Hess".

The summer of June 25, 1967 and had come and gone.

"The greatest glory in living lies not in never falling, but in rising every time we fall."
Nelson Mandela

CHAPTER 6
FALL OF 1967 — ELEVENTH GRADE

After this semester began, we were recording on Saturdays, the various schools would report on Sundays and on Monday mornings; I would walk into the auditorium chest out and full of myself. I overheard one of the popular boys, Larry Brown, speaking to someone about how mannish this person sounds. *"She sounds like a man, that Hester Johnson has the roughest voice and she sounds horrible."*

I was crushed when I heard Larry Brown laughing and telling the other cute boys how terrible, I sounded. I really thought that I was doing a good job and this popular boy was breaking me down. I took a seat, did not say a word and began to doubt myself every time I was on the radio.

The first day of school was spent discussing who had gotten pregnant, who wasn't coming back and a rumor that a teacher at our school had impregnated a student and the parents of the girl forced the teacher to marry the student or lose his job. This story was the top story on the minds of the Carver Cobras for a long time.

Some of the girls talking smack were Charlotte White, Brenda Smith and Beverly Warren; they were speaking and acting like pros. These girls took class with me and we were the same age. I had to watch it. I mean you had to think about sex because we talked about sex so much. I was not giving up any because I was scared that if I did, I would surely get pregnant. I was seeing this boy Charles off and on since the eighth grade. Mostly I saw him at school and our *relationship* had pretty much simmered down by this time. He told me later. *"I was just another silly girl."*

We would mostly grind and kiss but nothing major happened until later. After I turn 15 and could receive company, I wasn't as interested in him anymore. He was old news. But it didn't' stop him for trying to get in my bloomers. He was constantly bugging me about giving him some and he always showed me a condom. I was scared to death. I knew my Mama would kill me if I got pregnant.

As days went by this same boy would come over to the school pleading to be my boyfriend; that he was serious about being serious but after years of playing around, I wasn't interested in him like I had been when I was younger. There were some things about him that I did like besides him being a bad boy. He was poplar, came from a good family, went to college and his eyes, oh my! His squinting eyes were mesmerizing and he could sweet talk up stuff like nobody else I ever met. I was a little afraid about being alone with him, not that he would hurt me but that he would talk me into to giving it up. I did not think I could resist him.

I kept him at bay as long as I could. I knew it would not be hard for me going out with him if I wanted to do it, but I was still scared. I wavered back and forth. Wanting to be grown but still a scared child in many ways. Mama was ready for me to start having company. She seemed to trust me doing errands for her, having to travel downtown alone and handling some of the family's personal business. Being sixteen, feeling like I am almost there. It was exhilarating. Graduating the following year was almost here.

Then Charles Moore came over to my house unannounced. I was petrified! No boy had ever dropped by house unannounced. I was like, *"How did he know where I lived, he has a lot nerve, he's old and my Mama is going to figure that out. What do I do?"* To my surprise, he knocked on my door and asked for me. I saw him from the middle room window walking up the street but had no idea that he was coming to visit me. My mother did not know that I had been messing around with Charles. I had never had him over nor

introduced him to her. This was huge mistake on his part. He came up and knocked on the door! I was shooing my Mama towards the door to tell her to tell him that I wasn't there. She said that she was not gonna lie for me but she said something that I never heard her say before me. *"She is in exposed."*
"Huh? In pose to what?" Charles said.
She said it again, *"Inexposed. You will have to come back another time."*
Puzzled, he said, *"I'll wait."* As if he would wait for me to become exposed. My mama closed the door. Not willing to take no for an answer, he hesitated momentarily then left. I couldn't believe he stood on the porch after my Mama closed the door. The nerve of him! I could not believe that he knew where I stayed anyway and at this time, I did not want to have anything to do with him. He walked away toward Trigg Street with his head held proud as if to say, *"no biggie"*.

How would I describe him? Arrogant, full of himself, self-centered, He would have the nerve to tell girls ok if you won't give me your number, take mine. Boys didn't do that.

The boy always called on the girl. He was the first that I knew would do that. He was smart, sex crazy and had lots of girlfriends. At least that's what I heard.

My Mama asked me, *"Why does he walk like that?"* As if, he was walking cool. She did not know that Charles had lost his leg playing football for Carver High School. Charles, was a junior and star running back, when another player spiked his leg. I never knew the whole story on the why's and why not's. It seems strange, now but I never asked. Charles was taken off the field as his leg hung from the stretcher. Days later his injury was severe enough that infection set in and the doctors were unable to save his leg. The doctors informed his parents that they would have to amputate. Charles later told me that he wanted to die rather than have his leg amputated. Wearing his fake leg caused him to limp as if he was walking cool. It did not stop him from getting the girls though. I heard that I was just one of many.

Now that I am 16, I believed that he would be able to talk me out of some stuff, like my clothes, so I did my best to avoid him. He had already left Carver High School and was in college at Memphis State. I felt he was too much for me to handle. If he was to start visiting, me at home, that would mean we would become an item and I could not deal with that.

PARTICIPATION AT SCHOOL

Earlier that summer, I had overheard my brother Jerry, talking to Mama about our lack of participation in any after school curriculum.

My brother, Jerry was a hot shot. He graduated from college and had the respect of all in our close-knit neighborhood. He made sure that we read something every day. If he was reading the newspaper, he insisted that we read the newspaper. I never talked on the telephone when he was around because he knowing that I was interested in boys would have gotten me a lashing from him or my Mama. The oldest brothers and sister did have permission to whip us if we got out of line.

The only other person that I knew in our neighborhood that went off to college was Booth Grice but due to some unforeseen circumstances, I don't think he finished. When he attended Lemoyne Owens, Jerry popularity shot up even more after his selection of Mr. Lemoyne. The student body even gave him a nickname Ajax, which he wore proudly. He did his student teaching at Booker T. Washington School. Unfortunately, he was unable to find employment in Memphis so he moved and taught in Philadelphia.

However, like most young Black men he was drafted in the army to serve in Vietnam. After his duty, he came back to Memphis and again was not able to find a job. My Mama did what my Mama would have expected anyone to do, she went to Memphis City Hall and found The Reverend James Netters which was also a city councilman. She complained that Jerry was unable to find a job and asked him to use his influence to get him employment. And indeed, he did. Jerry worked for over 42 years and retired from Memphis City Schools.

Jerry always said he felt as if he was on a slave plantation and education would be a sure ticket of escaping poverty.

I listened to him from another room as he pleaded with my mother to act upon getting the younger brother and sisters involved in other activities. He was so passionate about his campaign. I listened and was moved by his pleas to Mama. She listened but never said anything to me about anything that Jerry had talked about.

I said to myself before summer is over and my 11th grade year, I will become involved but with what? I never saw myself as a sports person but I love playing softball on the Kansas Street Park. Jerry the park manager had done a wonderful job with his sisters and brothers and the neighborhood kids teaching us how to play various sports but the sports that he taught us were limited to softball and tennis. Tennis seemed like a good sport but we did not have a tennis team at Carver High School.

School started in September; I am going to make an effort to participate in extra activities. I listened to Jerry's plea and decided with or without my Mama's blessing, I would sign up for something. School had started. All of the 1967 seniors had left. The 1968 seniors were in full rare form but before I could sign up for anything, I did something stupid in the eyes of a teacher.

These bad girls were in the bathroom cutting class and one of them came up with an idea to put our little hair we had on our head in a pixie. We were imitating Tabitha on the television show *Bewitched*. It seemed harmless so I decided to join the five girls in the bathroom. Cute, I thought. One by one, we filed out of the bathroom. We looked around to see who was looking at us as we strolled down to the cafeteria. This was the same group of girls that brought an empty bottle of gin to the bathroom. The leader dared all of us to take a swig and we did. Yep, I took a swig to. Lord knows if my Mama had found out, I would have been dead meat.

As we walked in the cafeteria, all eyes were on us. We were cool. We snickered some, then ordered lunch. I can remember Mrs.

Tennessee, one of the cafeteria managers asking us *"What the hell yawl doing."*

Then a student came to us as we were eating to say that Miss Joan Johnson gym teacher wanted to see us in the gym. *For what?* Someone said, if a teacher asked to see you, you just went and dared not to go. So the five us strolled to the gym. Joan Johnson was standing on the stage with her hands on her hip.

Joan Johnson was built. She had a figure that had no fat attached anywhere to her body. She was tough and did not take anything from any student. She watched as we all filed in the gym. Standing before her as she stood on stage elevated to us. She gave a stern look and opened her mouth, *"What the hell yawl doing,"* she demanded. *"What is that shit in your hair? What are you trying to prove?"* We all stood there waiting to answer although we knew we could not answer. *"You look a mess, and you need to sit down and quit trying to be somebody which you aren't. Who are you trying to be."*

"We fixed our hair like Tabitha on Bewitch," someone said. "What? That white girl doesn't care nothing bout yawl ass and you need to be somewhere trying to make something out of yourself," she told us. "I'm surprised at you Hester Johnson." We mumble something after she tore us down and then said, "Get out of here, you make me sick, you ain't gonna ever be anything. And take your hair down!" We all quietly exit the gym with one hand toward our pixie. Charlsey Bell and her sister Bernice said, "Fu***k her. She ain't our Mama." I took mine down but the others said, "She can't do nothing to us."

I took P.E. from Joan Johnson but never had any direct dealing with her. I exercised, did what I was told and left. I felt terrible! Especially on the comment she made that we would not amount to anything. We just put our hair in a pixie and we thought it was cute.

One day Barbara Thompson, a twelfth grader and beauty queen with four of her friends ran to me excitedly explaining that Joan Johnson, was looking for dancers for her outside organization J.U.G.S a nonprofit organization that selected girls to solicited ads from businesses and each year during a gala these girls would present wearing elaborate costumes representing that company. These girls were called **Living Ads**.

Once she had an example of her girls dancing at Carver, one of the girls was from Booker T Washington high school, Francis Cook. Wow, she could dance. I wanted to dance like her and when Jeanette and Ruth Sharpe (sisters) from Carver danced, I was hooked. They were living ads and they put a show on unlike anything I had ever seen.

I was scared to death to go to Joan Johnson to asked whether I could participate. If it involved money, I already knew that that was out. My Mama didn't have money to waste as she put it. I thought to myself Joan Johnson would see that I can dance and that I wanted to make something out of myself. I hesitated a bit. Then cute Shirley Morman, Kat, and Barbara said, *"Look we will go with you and tell her that you can dance. Please…!!! OK lets go."* They tugged at me pulling on my arm all the way to the gym.

When we arrived their were girls from Carver and neighboring schools standing around. I guess that they had been invited to audition. I later found out Barbara and her crew had been asked to dance but they weren't interested in participating. So here we are, surrounded by these girls and my crew expressing with great enthusiasm to Joan Johnson that I could really dance! Joan Johnson responded with a disdainful look on her face, "*I know her*". I stood there like a fool waiting for her to say ok show me what you got. She did not. I looked around and saw girls with long beautiful hair, light skin and pretty. I never saw myself as pretty but thought I would do until the next girl came along. She refused their request and sent me on my way. I said to myself. "*She hates me.*" Wow, I was crushed. I tried. My friends tried. So what's next?

    I still felt compelled to heed my brother's cry that we needed to participate in extra activities to make him or my Mama proud. I so wanted to feel some appreciation and recognition of my talents and efforts. The opportunity finally came to dance as a go-go girl by way of a boy from Melrose High School. Anthony Taylor was the lead guitarist with *"The Chapango's."* A rock soul band of about six boys dressed in gold lamae ultra shiny jumpsuits. They were the bomb. We had three invitations to dance at the Veteran Hospital, Carver High School and Lemoyne Owens College's Magicians Basketball game. My Mama gave her okay and I was in like Flynn.

The Shindig at the Veterans Hospital was attended by men dressed in hospital gowns that looked like that were zoned out. No one really whooped and hollered or even looked like they were there. *The Chapangos* gave them there all and the go-go girls shook our shimmy but it was eerie.

The second Shindig took place at Carver High School. I was nervous but I was on Cloud nine to perform for my school. The crowd went wild. I bumped, shook, shimmied, and waved my arms; prancing from one end of the stage to the other. This was heaven. Afterward, the show was over, a couple of teachers wanted to know why would I do such a thing. Dancing like a wild woman on that stage and saying it was not a good look for the Cobras. I couldn't win for losing. I loved to dance.

The third invitation didn't fare so well. We all showed up, *The Chapangos* and the go-go girls. We were early and waited for instructions. Halftime was designated for *The Chapangos*; only to be told, *"No thank you."* We were not performing! *"Sorry."* The place was pack. *"Dang!"* The instruments were in and the go-go girls were ready. All I could do was watch the game and wait on my Mama to pick me up.

Next, I joined the Thespian Guild with Mr. Goddard. We never did anything but take a picture in the 1967-68 yearbook. We didn't compete with other schools or do any plays. You were required to take Mr. Goddard's class if you wanted to be in the Thespian Guild. That was a joke. Mr. Goddard was a high yellow, tall and arrogant teacher that did not teach. We spent most days with Mr. Goddard scoring on anybody and everybody in class while he sent the boys on errands that required leaving campus to go to the corner store for him. We suspected that he was a little sweet but couldn't' prove it. Brenda Smith and Mr. Goddard would have harsh war of words scoring on each other. She was a student that would lash back at him if he called her a name and she would call him *"flat ass."* The class would roar with laughter and sometimes he was outdone, Mr. Goddard would give a half smile because the score was funny.

I had never heard a student and teacher talk like that but it seems that he enjoyed these episodes. I stayed out of his way after he told me that *the back of my curly hair looked like a chicken's ass.* That was it for me. I was very embarrassed. I never said too much. I was attempting to become involved in activities that would make my Mama and brother proud. Being in the Thespian Guild seemed to be a good idea but it wasn't rewarding.

I WASN'T GIVING UP

I liked the look of the ROTC Sponsors. This group of girls was part of the ROTC team for the boys. The boys wore army green color uniforms. This group of boys were very serious about being in ROTC. However, the girl's uniforms were snazzy. The red jackets were tight fitting with gold double breast gold buttons. An ascot looped around the neck. A rope swung over your rotary cup and bars pinned to your left breast. The skirts were also tight fitting and the length came to the knee. We all had to wear black pumps with hose, white gloves and a red tam. The girls marched with precision; eyes forward and very military. You took this job serious and you had up and coming **Sponsors** looking up to you.

All incoming ninth graders boys were required to sign up for ROTC. The girls however had to go out or audition to be a Sponsor. Joan Johnson did not have a hand in the Sponsors, so I went out, I show up for try-outs. You had to remember the cadences, you needed to be able to stand at attention and having a pretty shape was a plus, I did have a small waistline and big legs. I was committed.

I never missed a practice. Although practice did not determine your selection but showing up every day and remembering the cadences were vital.

The day came for the eliminations. I was ready because I was able to follow the commands, showed up every day and I was determined. We all lined up at attention, eyes forward. The commander and high-ranking boys in ROTC were standing on a ledge leading from the gym. As they looked us over. I saw someone that looked familiar. *Oh my God!!!!* I said to myself. Out of the corner of my right eye, I saw her! Joan Johnson! I was hoping that she did not see me. Then I heard this female voice *"I know that ain't Hester Johnson out there?* It was her, Joan Johnson!!!!!!

Poised and ready, I stayed at attention; eyes forward and hands to the side. The officers began to call names from a list; these names were the names of the ones that weren't selected for ROTC. I heard my name called from the list. ***"Hester Johnson."*** I was devastated. I had worked so hard. I was at every practice. I listened and took note that it was very importance to be able to stay at attention for long periods. I exited the line and like the other girls that weren't chosen, disappointed, I gathered my books and left.

I loved ROTC. I was not selected because of Mrs. Joan Johnson's dislike for me and not my ability. This time, I said to myself *"No"* I wouldn't tell my Mama, but the following day, I went to the commander and said *"Sir I really want to be a Sponsor. I have worked hard."* I was really nervous because I was disagreeing with a teacher that had power at this school, she was well respected and I was going against her decision. He looked at me and sternly then said *"I know Miss Johnson, and you are a ROTC Sponsor. Show up for practice today."* When I arrived for ROTC practice, scared to death, I filed in line. I didn't say a word. Some of the girls were staring at me and thinking, *"Her name WAS called on yesterday. Why is she here."*

The leaders began to call the roll of the typed names on this sheet of paper and could not find my name on the roster. The commander that was there asked the leader of the *Sponsors* to add my name. They all looked around at each other as if to say, "Wooowee. Joan Johnson ain't gonna like this," but they followed the Commanders orders.

From that unfortunate event, it was an uphill battle.

SECOND BATTLE

It was time to select a Miss ROTC. You could only be selected if you are in the eleventh grade so as to serve your senior year. I am in the eleventh grade; I will be a senior the following year, so I am sure that I qualify. I put my name in. Wrong thing to do.

The new teachers that were the ROTC sponsors wanted another young student to be Miss ROTC and this young lady had been a sponsor since tenth grade. I was just coming on board but still qualified. The votes were in. I won. The wrong person to win was me. Beverly should have won in the eyes of the teachers.

The teachers took upon themselves to say Beverly is the new Miss ROTC but the students' officers said that is not who they voted for. The teachers then demanded a second vote. Upsetting the lead student's officers, they campaigned to every ninth grader and to any boy that was in ROTC to vote for me. I won. Wrong person to win again.

The teachers now fuming that I won again and asked for another vote but this time the officers said *"No."* Let Mr. Thompson our principal come in and make the decision. All parties involved were there. Mr. Thompson gave his speech about what was the problem. The officers and head ROTC teachers spoke up. Mr. Thompson said, *"We don't have a problem if the vote of the officers voted for Hester Johnson. Hester Johnson you are the 1968-1969 Miss ROTC."*

The room erupted in a roar of hand clapping along with Beverly storming out with tears and our teacher sponsors mad as hell. Beverly was my friend and still is to this day. I did not know how to give up the title to someone that wanted it so badly. I wished that I didn't want it so badly but I did.

The ceremony given each year in Miss ROTC's honor was full of pageantry and recognition. The high ranking student ROTC officers would escort the girl sponsors bearing gifts to the newly elected Miss ROTC. The entire school would witness this gala affair as the new Miss ROTC was treated with royalty and high esteem as they had done in previous years.

This year however; the teachers decided that this event would no longer take place. I looked forward to this affair but in no way could I do anything about it. After all I was not the queen the teachers wanted and the majority vote did not matter to them.. I can truly say that I was disappointed but the madness didn't stop there. When homecoming day approach, each queen was expected to ride in the parade, waving to her adoring fans and community. I lost that opportunity too. The disappointed teachers allowed Beverly to ride in the parade (in a convertible car) unbeknownst to me. I was later asked *"where were you?"* I had no response, because I had deliberately not been told about any of the plans. I suspected that no one looked for me and had no intention of looking for me.

Oh well, even though I tried to participate so I could make my Mama and brother Jerry proud, it seemed like I was challenged on every front.

Trigg Avenue and Michigan Street ...the corner where I grew up

It all started at Carver High School

1968 Junior Year at Carver High

1969 Graduation

1968-69 Queen's Court: Juanita White, Sandra Grant, Hester Johnson, Arthur Smith and Miss Carver Carmen Griffin

April 1968
The Headline
That Stunned
The World

The Article in the Commercial Appeal was my first interview about my involvement in the 1968 Sanitation Worker's Strike.

Early 1990's plus size Model Orlando, FL

In the Spirit of Harriet in Minneapolis, MN

Footsteps Summer Youth Program in LeMoyne-Owen College Memphis, TN

Presentation at St. Francis Catholic School Greenwood, MS

April 4th Foundation Summer Youth Program Vision Board

April 4th Foundation Summer Youth Program

Kwanza Celebration

One Woman Show

Storyteller

El Centro College
Dallas, TX

2020 Photo Shoot

DFW Child Magazine
Summer Camp Program

16N68: MY STORY
SECTION THREE:
THE MARCH

"The time is always right to do what is right."
Dr. Martin Luther King, Jr.

CHAPTER 7
THE DAY EVERY THING CHANGED

The Porch Game

We had this one game, my sisters and I. Sometimes we would include a niece or two Audrey and Yvette, we were one blended family. The game went like this. Who is going to speak to the next person that would come by? It did not matter whether that person would speak to us first or not. On this particular day it was my turn. The very next person that would make his or her way around Trigg and Michigan and come toward us would be my person. It would be my turn to speak.

We saw this man and could not make out his face, but soon I realized that it was Mr. McGee. Mr. McGee was a garbage man and father to Roy and Wilma McGee; he and Mrs. McGee had other children but somehow I could never remember any of them but Roy and Wilma. Mr. McGee usually walked a little swiftly but this time his strive was a little off. The five of us; Peggy Audrey, Michaele, and Yvette said it about the same time *"Wonder what's wrong with Him?*

Hey Mr. McGee, I said loudly. He barely spoke. He tipped his hat and kept going. We didn't' say another word. We just watched as he slowly, passed by. We all looked at each other as we watch him stroll on down the street. Whoa, I felt bad for him. He looked sad and worn. Then we began to hear the talk about the sanitation strike. Obviously, the trash began to pile high in front of our house and the neighbors. We knew the men were on strike but somehow it did not faze us.

We did not have a front yard .Our house (a grey duplex) sat high up from the street as if the house was on stilts but not. We had a bird's eye view of activities way before anyone could reach our home. The gravel roadway was our sidewalk and the rocks met the street...so the sides of the road which were not a sidewalk also served as parking spaces for cars parking and a way to get out of the way when cars were passing by.

I later learned from his daughter, Wilma that her daddy had taken on another job at an icehouse. He was packing ice for delivery. This work occurred after a day of picketing during the day. Wilma also informed me that neighbors were always bringing food over.

The workers' wages were less than five dollars a week. Mr. Sam of Weona would deliver or have food delivered to their home on occasions. She said they never went hungry. She and her family were the only family on the whole street that had a father beside Bobby June's, daddy, Mr. Fred.

I guess the man was just tired. I had no way of knowing but he looked worn. The McGee lived on the end of Michigan Street near Olive Street, so the only time we would see the children if we walked that way to school or if we actually would see them at school. Somehow, the sanitation strike had not reached my radar until that day when I saw Mr. McGee for myself.

When the news got out that Dr. King was asked to come to shed some light on the situation or just to help out, then we began to hear the teachers, and community folks talking. My ears perked up. I wanted to help but did not see how I could? This seemed like such a grown-up thing.

The garbage stank. I mean it really was a problem. The garbage was piling up. It was getting to be a real nuisance because dogs normally roamed the streets, so the dogs began to destroy any thing that smelled like dinner to them. We did not have plastic bags. In my neighborhood that would have been a waste. Spending money on something that you were going to throw away seemed crazy. Everything went in the garbage, dead animals, human waste, spoiled food, sanitary napkins, you name it, and it ended in the hordes of garbage. The maggots and flies were another issue.

The year of 1968 was a time when music and knowing the latest dance moves was important to a Black girl in high school. You could not go the sock hop and not know how to dance. I knew how to dance, I love dancing, but I did not go to many sock hops if my Mama or my brothers had anything to do with it. If I asked to go to a sock hop and one of my brothers found out, they would get to my Mama before she could give me an answer. They grind on those girls' when the slow songs come on. They are going to try to grind on Hester and plus those dances are not for good girls. Well I saw the only way I could go to the sock hops was to sneak or go to the one that was held during the day. At 16 in 1968, I spent most of my time listening to Aretha Franklin, James Brown, and the Temptations.

    I was not concerned about a bunch of Black men walking off their jobs. Jobs were hard to find then in 1968 and men walking off their jobs to be treated like men was something I could not truly comprehend at 16. Nor was I discussing the situation with any of my family, friends or even the teachers at my school

Somehow seeing Mr. McGee made a complete difference in the way I saw things; it really hit close to home of what was going on. I never expected to see Dr. King or even be near...I knew if he came then it would put another complete spin on the situation. Like bringing others in on the strike and boycott. I did not have a concept of this but knew something would be different. I did not know how it would play out.

At my school B.J. Williams, an English teacher at George Washington Carver High School was no joke. B.J. Williams was a teacher from the old school. I dreaded having her for English and pitied anyone else who had to serve time taking English from her. Her eyes pierced through you like superman's ultra x-ray vision and if you tried to lie or were lying about something, she would tell you that you were lying even if you did not do it. There was no way out but her way. She made you believe that you did the crime anyway. Somehow, she thought I was a troublemaker. I had a huge afro and any girl that wore an afro back then had to be a troublemaker.

Mr. Thompson, our principal at Carver had already given his disapproval of me or any other girl wearing an afro. Matter of fact he once told me that he would not allow his sons to date a girl wearing one. Now that was a crusher because I had a lot of respect for Mr. Thompson and given the fact that I might lose a chance to date one his sons was a bummer.

BJ Williams was the first teacher that I heard speak against Dr. King coming to Memphis. She would fold her arms, speaking rapidly with this mean look on her face, *"He needs to mind his own business,"* shaking her head from side to side. *"We don't need trouble in Memphis."* I could not understand why she would be against Dr. King visit. *"They just garbage men. What's the fuss anyway."* It was if garbage men did not deserve representation.

We were always told in the classroom by teachers, *"don't get your lessons, and you gonna be digging ditches, or picking up garbage."* Well, I did not get it. I got it later. However, I did not understand why she would say such a thing. She kept ranting on *"He need to stay where he belongs. We don't want him here, there is nothing wrong here in Memphis that he thinks he can fix, he's just going to cause trouble."*

"I have learned over the years that when one's mind is made up, this diminishes fear."
Rosa Parks

CHAPTER 8
DR. KING COMES TO MEMPHIS

George Hunt, art teacher, track coach and eye candy to all the young girls at George Washington Carver High School and Miss Davis were in the hall talking. We had two Miss Davis, this was Irene Davis, she was a teacher that did not, and I repeat did not take any stuff at all. She wore an afro and was fairly radical.

I think R.B. Thompson, our illustrious principal had reprimanded Irene Davis about wearing her afro; at least that is the students heard. She wore her Afro anyway. She was loud, she sounded like us (hood) and she had a bounce in her walk. Radical, yes she was. Who asked, I do not remember. It could have been Mr. Dowdy; he was another art teacher that was somewhat outspoken. Matter of fact, Mr. Dowdy ran for president of the United States and he didn't win.

"*Do you want to participate in boycotting the stores downtown?*" one of them asked. I pause not knowing what was being asked of me. "*Not really,*" I thought to myself. He went on to say "*Dr. King has sent word that he wants more young people to participate in a movement that would affect their future. Are you interested?*"

Even though I was thinking not really. I said, "*Yes*" without any hesitation, not why? Like so many students do today; just yes. "*Yes, but I have to asked my mother. Would I have to do this during school hours?*" I do not even remember asking that question but I must have.

Mr. Hunt went on to say, "*Now the thing is you would have to attend non-violent training at Clayborn Temple before you can participate.*" Clayborn Temple a church where sanitation workers held their meetings, was owned by the African Methodists Episcopal Church. This is where the training will take place.

I just had to show up at a particular church that I never attended. I still said *"Yes."* God knows why, I don't remember asking my Mama, but she had to agree because I would need her to take me downtown but the bus system was going to be my primary mode of transportation.

Seem like she was beaming when I told her that I was asked by the teachers to participate as if I was special or something. I did not necessary feel special but I wanted to help especially since Dr. King sent the word to the ministers to get young people involved. And after seeing Mr. McGee, I wanted to be involved and this was a sure way to participate.

The day came for the first day of training and I remember there were kids from other schools. I was the only one from Carver. This is where I first met Ernestine Hunt, a 10th grader from Melrose High School. Ernestine is now a judge in Memphis and has been for quite some time. She was from a place that I had never been in Memphis, Orange Mound. Orange Mound was Black ran, Black owned and kicking ass in Orange Mound was no joke. If you did not live in the Mound, I do not think it would have been wise to be there at night.

We listened, to the preacher that was giving us instructions on what to do. One thing for sure, we could not travel alone. We always had to operate in pairs. Stay together! Then he began to scream at us. We were not doing anything wrong but he said this is what to expect but we would learn not to respond. We were there for a purpose. Keep our eyes forward. Do not look around. Stay focus. I do not remember how many days that took place. We had day duty and night duty.

The signs were passed out to all that were there. We were always attentive to what instructions were given to us. It was very important to take the lead of the adult person, no talking, no horsing around; this was serious, very serious. No talk of boys, no giggling, no whose dating who, I took this serious and we had to be serious. I never ever thought about how this would look to my friends. Nor did I wonder what all those boys

I that I spoke of earlier would think of me. Those thoughts didn't cross my mind. I was on a mission to try and make a difference. This whole process was serious, so I was serious. Over and over, the pastors were constantly drilling it in us how serious our jobs were.

Anyone that knows me even now knows that I love to laugh, holler, cut up and sometimes act a fool, but during this period I was eyes front listening to every command and always watchful.

MY FIRST DAY TO PICKET

We assembled in front of Clayborn Temple. We were given our signs. Did we walk up there or did we go by car. I cannot remember. We assembled in front of Goldsmiths Department store. I shopped there for my Mama many times, at least in the basement. You felt kind of eerie shopping on the upper floors, the whites would stare at you hard. Most of our purchases came from the basement where the sales were. I knew my place and never mentioned to anyone that I swiped a spool of thread from Goldsmith. I was simply mortified, that my Mama would kill me if she knew that I did not pay for it. I put the thread in my pocket and held on to it with all my might. I wanted to take it back but then I was too scared to. Lord knows I was terrified of taking that spool of thread.

Now I am back to boycott the very story I had taken a spool of thread from. What if someone remembers me from that day; the day that I took that spool of thread. They told us that we could not block the door. Stay on the sidewalks. Keep walking and keep singing. Eyes straight. We could not make direct contact with customers but we could shout out and sing. We would always take the lead person, starting a song and then we would begin singing that song. *I AIN'T GONNA LET NOBODY TURN ME AROUND, OH FREEDOM, WE SHALL OVERCOME*. I do not enjoy that last song.

I am like Dr. King in one of his speeches. HOW *LONG LORD? HOW LONG?* **MY FIRST PUBLIC ENCOUNTER.**

We were up by Three Sisters, a department store about 10 stores from Goldsmiths. It was a tight corner to turn. We were singing; carrying our signs and watching for instigators. An elderly white woman, about 80-years-old, abruptly stopped as I was about to pass her. Arms folded, she parked on top of newspaper stand and began mumbling. I could not make out what she was saying but I could see that she was angry; and the picketers had said nothing to her. I know that I had not said anything to her.

My Mama always taught us to be respectful to old people and she was no different. She said *"Nigga gwon home...gwon home nigga,"* and before I knew it she spat on my shoulder! My nostrils flared open but I took a deep breath. I tensed up but kept my eyes forward; taking another deep breath, I actually felt sorry for her. She had no clue that we were not going to leave. I was not going anywhere. I was staying put and I kept walking. I was shocked to say the least. I remember thinking oddly that her glasses seemed to be glued to her face. She looked flustered and worried. She hesitated some and slowly stepped away repeating *Niggas, Niggas go home.*

The Black folks would hold their heads down when they would pass us. It was like they were saying, *"Do what you have to do and we are going to do what we are going to do."* Walk in this store...it was as if they were in sympathy with us, but yet still going in the stores. If we had to leave or if we became tired, we could not leave the march alone. It did get tiresome. We were always ever watching for unmarked cars. The white men with dark suits sitting in these white cars with no signal on them. They usually wore black suits and a hat, and smoke filled the cars while they just starred at us. The preachers taught us to look for unmarked cars. We could not show any fear, but at least we wanted them to know that we saw them and they wanted us to know they were looking at us. We were told that we all were being investigated or somehow had our names written down for later. I needed to leave so one of leader asked someone to stay with me until I got on the 12 Florida bus to go home. This boycotting marching took place during the day.

At night we only marched up to a certain time ... each time we had to come back to turn in our signs one by one. I am sure one of the ministers brought me home. I was hoping that it would not be Pastor Brown. There was something about him and his flirtation ways that made me uncomfortable. It did not help that he was this small framed little preacher with large big brown eyes. He was creepy. He spoke kind of low and in what he thought was an enticing way. His white collar was always starch and extremely white. He was always skinning and grinning talking out the side of his mouth. I stayed clear of him because he flirted with the young girls, which I thought was out of place. I was leery of him. He was always asking for hugs and I was not about to give him one. I really wanted to be here but not at the expense of having to give a slimy preacher a little kiss and big hug. I stayed clear of him and his flirty ways. *I DID NOT WANT HIM COMING NEAR ME!*

I didn't tell my Mama because I knew that would be trouble, trouble. I never ever told her about Pastor Brown asking me for a kiss. I never hugged him in the way he wanted me too like the other girls. He even referred once before that I thought I was too good to hug and/or kiss him. I was too good.

BACK AT SCHOOL

B.J. Williams pulled me to side. *"I hear that you may be involved in something way over your head...that you are being a troublemaker."* I never got into trouble in school and I did not feel like I was doing wrong. Missing a couple of days out of school but over the radio, WDIA and WLOK the black stations; the adults were saying this was the sacrifice that we had to make to help end this strike.

My mama did not mind. Matter of fact my Mama never had to come over to the school for me anyway so that was not unusual that she would say anything. She taught us how to behave and sent us on our way to do the right thing especially since she was still whipping butt at 16.

I listened to mean ass B.J. Williams. There was no cause to be disrespectful and I would not be anyway. She really did not know what she was talking about and I did not want to hear it nor explain to her any differently. I nodded my head (yes ma'am) and went on my way.

After the boycotting started we began to hear more about the situation in our city. We even had days that we the student body showed solidarity. At 12 noon, all students would stand, hands to the side, and the teachers stepped out of the room with no words spoken. One by one, we would stand, and then the next and the next until all students stood to show the support for the workers that were on strike. At 12:01, the teacher would step back into the room and continue class as if nothing happened. That was *powerful seeing all the students standing together!*

The songs were embedded in my head: **HOLD ON, AIN'T GONNA LET NOBODY**

TURN ME AROUND and *KEEP YOUR EYES ON THE PRIZE!*

There were other freedom songs to get us by during the day; to help keep us revved up for the hours of marching. This time we were going to line up and march at night. Again we assembled in front of the Clayborn Temple heading to Goldsmith. You really could not see the faces as well at night but the message was the same. *NO SHOPPING HERE! KEEP YOUR MONEY IN YOUR POCKET!*

Then we would sing the songs over and over again. We were hoping that at least Black folks would not go in the stores. We were instructed again to not block the entryways, keep eyes front and allow the lead person to start a song.

EYES FORWARD!

KEEP YOUR EYES ON THE PRIZE!

HOLD ON!

Was I scared? Yeah, I was very scared, was I ready to give my life to this cause? No. I knew I had a right to be here and I thought I would be protected by the adults. I would march and then go home. Just like before. I would do the right thing and then go home. Parked by Gayosa Street would be a plain car with white men. Always two white men, wearing sunglasses and smoky faces; taking long draws from cigarettes. These cars were unmarked cars watching us. We checked for the license plates. If the plates started with G and numbers we knew it was a government vehicle.

WATCH AND REMEMBER!

NEVER LEAVE THE MARCH ALONE!

ALWAYS TRAVEL IN PAIRS!

That was an instruction that was familiar. My mama always told us to travel in pairs and why? If something happened to one or the other of us, the one can run and tell. It should work the same here. Believe me I never asked her why. We knew there would be times when those directions would pay off. This thing is getting serious now, garbage was everywhere and the stench was almost unbearable. We left day in and day out to school amidst piles and piles of garbage.

Now we are getting ready for the big day. Dr. King had agreed to come. The organizers got us involved as Dr. King asked. We are getting ready for the big march with Dr. Martin Luther King, Jr. This is huge. He agreed to come to Memphis. I must say I was very nervous yet excited. He will see that we can participate in this thing and not go hog-wild crazy. It was not a lot of young people but enough that he would see that work had been done with no incidents while picketing downtown.

"My humanity is bound up in yours, for we can only be human together."
Desmond Tutu

CHAPTER 9
THE NIGHT BEFORE IT ALL WENT WRONG

I remembered the night before; I was like I got this. My afro and huge sunglasses, dashiki and jeans were laid out. At least I will be fashionable. I did not think of the magnitude of 1300 men walking off their jobs. Moreover, the greatness of this strike. I wanted others to see that young people were part of this, but I still wanted an opportunity to look good. I was piddling around most of the morning at home and did not sleep well the night before. The adults had asked us to get there early. I guess to show the work that had been done.

I arrived and there were seas of seas of Black folks there, young and old. I saw eyes on me, like who is she. I would not dare go to the front. I was supposed to go up front to be near Dr. King but I was too emotional to do it. I saw these men running back and forth, screaming,

"GET IN LINE!"

We were to line up with eight across then 16 across. Eyes forward, get in line. They were screaming in our ears as they did in training. I was accustomed to this.

"GET IN LINE!"

People were talking and not singing. I did not see a soul from George Washington Carver High School, nor anyone of the students from the training, so I just stood in front of Clayborn Temple until someone told me to get in line! We began to hear reports that young people were walking off the campus of various schools; pouring out into the streets. Then we heard that Hamilton High students were hurling rocks at passing cars that white folks were driving. Humes Junior High School students walked out. They were walking out of schools unsupervised. Ranting and heading toward downtown, others marchers became antsy. We heard these stories and somehow were glad that they were walking out but quite upset that trouble was brewing unsupervised.

I felt like I wanted to stand-out but I knew that I was one of hundreds yet I felt different, special, like I had gone through training just for this special day. I was prepared. It was a cloudy day, it looked like rain, a man ran franticly to the back of the line. He's here! He's here! Dr. King is here! Dr. King is here…." Then others began to whisper like turning their heads to the wind over their shoulders….He's here…He"s here..it was like it was not real.

"He's here, I said to myself,, He's here… he did come….He's here…. I tightly closed my eyes…dreaming like. Unbelievable that he came…and I began to softly cry. I began to cry harder. The greatness of it all and what we were doing hit me hard as I stiffen my body and began to sing along...Most of us sang but not all.

We Shall Overcome. We Shall Overcome. However, others were still talking as if we had not pushed off.

"STAY IN LINE! STAY IN LINE!"

The grown men would frantically pass by almost pushing us back in line.

"STAY IN LINE!"

It seemed a bit uneasy; the marchers were walking and talking. I had an uneasy feeling but could not pinpoint exactly what those feelings where. *"Why aren't they singing? This is not the way we were trained."* People were talking and not singing. Someone pushed me. The crowd began pushing and coming very close to one another. Then there was this loud rushed voice.

Someone screamed. Then again and again. Then...

"STAY IN LINE! STAY IN LINE!"

I looked around. Confused. Someone ahead and someone behind screamed with a shrieking sound of panic. The voice screamed again and then we all began a slow shuffling run. We stated to rush toward Beale Street. Then there was the sound of gunfire, and cries of panic filled the air. Then shouts of ...

"RUN! RUN! RUN!"

Windows were being broken. More screams filled the air! Then we started running in the direction in which we were headed. Everyone was freaking out. I began looking for instructions. There was much pushing and confusion.

"OH MY GOD!"

"NO NO!" I said to myself. *"NO! NO! NO!"* then I shouted out loud.

"THIS IS NOT WHAT DR.KING WANTED!"

I found myself in front of a music store.

"DON'T DO THIS!
DON'T DO THIS!
THIS IS NOT WHAT DR. KING WANTED!" I screamed.

At that moment a huge two-by-four flew past my head. I didn't know where the board came from. It didn't matter. Fortunately I was able to duck or I would have been hit hard, ***very hard.*** My hands landed on solid concrete covered with broken glass. Then there was the sound of gunfire again, and the screaming of terrified people in a crazy panic. As I stood up I repeated,

"THIS IS NOT WHAT DR. KING WANTED!"

I fell to my knees. I felt as if my head was about to explode. Blood, blood and more blood was everywhere. Something nicked the side of my hands. I was bleeding. On my knees, screaming!

"NO! THIS IS NOT WHAT DR. KING WANTED! STOP DOING THIS! NO, NO!"

I buried my head between my knees. More glass shattering. There were more screams and sirens. Many police officers arrived swinging sticks. Then, I heard a man's voice,

"RUN! RUN! GO BACK TO THE CHURCH!!"

I searched for the voice and saw a man covering his nose and mouth with a handkerchief, while pointing in the direction of the church. It was one of the pastors. *"Run back to the church!"*

"God help us. Oh God help me." The sound of the breaking of the glass would forever be etched in my mind. Looking from side to side around me, there were many people bleeding, and a frightening deathly panic set in. I ran as fast as I could back to the church.

"Run! Run! Run!"
Screams
Pushing
Terror
Gunshots
More screams
Police
Mace
Eyes burning
This is not what Dr. King wanted

I saw friends at the church, Suzette Sanders, Robert and Pugh. We were all crying. We all rushed into the church, not knowing what to do. As we stood in the aisle, bewildered, confused and scared. Our eyes burned from the mace and tear gas.

The pastor asked us to go up to the balcony. I screamed, *"I know we are going to die! Dr. King did not want this and my Mama ain't going to know where to pick me up!"*

My desperate thought was that if I died, my Mama wouldn't know where to find me! *"We are dead!"* I repeatedly shouted. *"We are dead!"* I kept repeating that over and over, *"We are dead!"*

Suzette shook me! Violently *"Shut Up! We ain't gonna die girl!!!! We ain't going to die.!!!"*

The mace in our face was way too much to handle. We covered our eyes, our mouths, and we were coughing uncontrollably. Children were laid out on the floor in front of the altar as thought they were dead. More children were brought in and laid at the altar. Oh my God! This chaotic scene was unbelievable! I never in my life had seen anything like this!!! *God help us. God help us!* The younger children were brought in the arms of older children. Some of the adults brought in appeared to be dead. They too were put at the altar; most had fainted or where knocked out cold by the crowd or the mace.

"What are we gonna do? I don't want to die!" The pastor was waving his hands for control. *"Please calm down. Calm down,"* he kept repeating. *"Calm down."*

John Ferguson a young adult, a loose cannonball, radical, and dangerous older teen was ranting around saying mothefu**** in church. John Ferguson was wild, crazy and cussed like a sailor. He lived near me but in another neighborhood. Somewhere off Florida Street, near Crump. He had long shoulder length straight hair. Not looking like the Negros I knew, he wore thick glasses and was loud and scary. He had a brother that looked just like him. Black brothers that were a cross between Chinese, Black and Native American. He was ranting as if he was going to do something crazy, ranting and stomping his feet. John was clinching his fists and had this crazed look on his face, he was out of control. Waving his hands and walking up and down the aisle of the church yelling *"kill, kill, kill!"*

The pastor pleaded with John to calm down. "Please calm down son." The pastor begged others for calmness. Children were still crying and some had not come to. The pastor asked others to go to the balcony. Several of us in the balcony looked out of the top window. Police had surrounded the church. Suddenly we heard a bullhorn coming from outside. *"This is the police!"* someone shouted.

"15 minutes! 15 minutes! You have 15 minutes to come out with your hands up!!!! I looked out from the balcony windows, and it seemed like hundreds of police officers were lined up with guns pointing toward the church. John Ferguson became enraged! He began to rant again! *"Kill the motherf***! Kill the motherf***. We ain't done nothing!"*

The pastor again beg for calmness and asked us to obey. *"Please! Please!"* he begged. Then again we heard, *"15 minutes or we are coming in. Come out with your hands up!!!* The pastor beckoned us from upstairs and we all gathered around him for a quick prayer. The pastor gave a quick prayer and once again pleaded with us to obey the police.

"Please!" he kept begging, *"do what the police say!"*

"You got to go through the going through to get through."
                                    H.O. Johnson

CHAPTER 10
ARE WE GONNA DIE?

The booming voice spoke again once the doors of the church opened. ***"Hands in the air! Hands in the air!*** While facing the police holding guns, my stomach was churning like crazy. I was so weak and speechless. ***"You go to the left and you go to the right!"*** They were splitting up our group. I immediately realized if I turned to the right then I would be going further into downtown, away from where I should be heading. And if I turned to the right then turn to the left, I thought that I would surely be shot. I turned to the left. I took a deep breath. Look at the sun of the directions that I came from I said to myself. ***"Go to the left. Stay left. Go back in the way*** *you came from!"* I kept saying that to myself over and over. *"Go back in the way that you came from."*

Guns with bayonets were pointed directly at our heads. The eyes of these men looked frightening and intense. We departed from the church like prisoners of war. My stomach was cramping and hurting and my face was solemn with no sudden movement.

Blank faces
Guns with bayonets
Suzette and I went to the left
Robert and Pugh went to the left
No words spoken
No talking was allowed
Just the sounds of silence...debris blowing in the wind
We all felt like we were prisoners of war

We had cried so long and hard that there were no words left in us. We walked some and then began to talk softly. We never said anything that I remember like, *"did you see this or did you see that?"* It was like we were mapping our way back home...so we had to be careful to stay on course...we were more concern about getting home than anything else.

We wrapped around Main Street to Crump Street, we knew to go left on Florida Street. I had taken the 12 Florida bus many times heading downtown and knew I was heading home, it was just such a long walk! We chatted a little bit until we got to Kroger's bakery.

This is an area that my mother never let me walk down to alone. We didn't know anyone on this side of Florida but we heard this was a bad end. The kids that lived on this end cursed in public. I knew two in particular, two sisters, two half white sisters that were about 6 feet tall. Nancy was the oldest, I was afraid of her and her sister was my age. They were rough, cursed in public and did not take any stuff from nobody. They even walked like thugs, and they lived on this end of Florida Street where I would never be caught walking alone. We walked on anyway. We came up to two boys that I recognized from school. I didn't know their names but recognized them. They were bad-ass boys and they knew we were not from the neighborhood. We kept on walking.

Hey, bitch! Nobody stopped. All of us kept walking. *"I'm talking to the Bitch with the glasses on."* I was the only one with glasses on so I knew he was talkin' to me. I softly said, *"Hello."* I quickly said, *"Hello"* again and kept looking forward. I was attempting to walk off when he walked up to me right in my face and slapped me so hard my glasses fell to the ground. *"Any you mother*****want to do anything about this?"* No one said a word. I was stunned, frozen as tears ran down my cheeks. Stunned, I just stared at him with stern emotions; my eyes and nose flared in and out, but not speaking. And in that instance, he kissed me on my mouth and pushed me down on the sidewalk. Then he yelled, *"Go on Bitch! You ain't nothing!"*

The boys with me did absolutely nothing! Not one word did they say. Suzette took me by my shoulders as she picked up my glasses from the ground. None of us said a word. I was boiling on the inside, but I couldn't speak. I remember thinking to myself, *"We just had guns pointed in our faces and now this!"* I was lost for words. We did not talk about what had just occurred. No one said one word.

Finally, we made it to Trigg and Florida. I live at Trigg and Michigan. The others lived near the school so we parted at Trigg. I repeatedly kept saying to myself those boys had no idea what we just went through. I never told my bad brother Ollie Kirk and I never told my Mama. Later, I only spoke about the incident when I did school presentations.

I never knew the bad boy's name. After the incident, I saw him with other bad boys from that area. I remember seeing him once when he walked past me, as though I was invisible, he never said a word. I didn't either. I didn't say one word. I noticed he had this slight limp. Someone told me later that the limp was the result of him having the claps. I quietly smiled to myself that he deserved catching a disease. I guess in my mind this was his punishment for assaulting me.

Often time my young audience think that these were white boys but they were not. We did not have white kids at our school or in our neighborhood. But sometimes white women and men would secretly sneak around to "visit" the Black men and women in our area during the night. When mixed-race children were born, we knew that some hanky panky had been going on in our neighborhood. Nothing like that went on in the daytime. We did not see any mixing of the races during the day.

I am tired and weary, humiliated and hungry. I made my way to the house, and planted myself in a chair that we always kept on the porch for Mama. I remember that I was quiet. I didn't say a word to my Mama. I had all kinds of emotions and fear built up inside of me. I didn't tell her that I was in all of that march mess downtown that she was now witnessing on The Walter Cronkite News. I could hear the news blasted in the front room.

My Mama was in full form. She was screaming Jubilee. I couldn't understand why she was so darn happy. I wondered to myself if she knew what just happened in downtown Memphis that we had guns pointed at our heads. I did not tell her that but I wanted her to see the anguish on my face. She never asked me *"What's wrong, or how are you doing. Did you get caught up in all that mess?"* Then she said something that solidified why she was so happy. She kept repeating, *"Walter Cronkite is talking bout Memphis!' We important! Walter Cronkite talking bout Memphis! Now they gonna do something! If Walter Cronkite talking bout us in Memphis, they gonna do something."*

She was dancing around, she was shouting *"Hallejulah!"* And she still did not asked me anything.

"What happened to Dr. King, What happen?" I said that to myself over and over again. *"I'm so mad!"* I kept hearing that song. *"Ain't gonna let nobody turn me around...I am gonna keep my eyes on the prize ...Hold on! Baloney!!! It all felt like a big joke."*

The next day the morning newspaper, *The Commercial Appeal* ran a cartoon in the paper of a gorilla gathering up her wayward babies. I would never forget that cartoon. It was portraying Dr. King as a mother gorilla being unable to keep his baby gorillas together.

Just like all the previous bad experiences I buried it deep inside and kept going.

"There are still many causes worth sacrificing for, so much history yet to be made."
First Lady Michelle Obama

CHAPTER 11
THE DAY DR. MARTIN LUTHER KING, JR. WAS ASSASSINATED

April 4th

I was trying to return to normal and get my life back. Like most sixteen-year-olds, I wanted to learn how drive. I really didn't have anything to drive but learning to drive was a major deal for a high school girl. Taking drivers education meant taking drivers classes at the Memphis Board of Education clear across town. I would come up with these wild ideas and I would figure out later how I was going to get there and get back home. We only had one car to a family of 10 brothers, sisters, nephews, nieces plus cousins. Rumor had it that it was always best to date a boy that had a car or drove his family car. I did not have a steady boyfriend at the time; although I was scouting. That would be a sure way of learning how to drive. Your boyfriend would teach you. I had been on and off again with this older guy Charles. He was still living with his parents so maybe he could pick me up. He was a "manish one" if you know what I mean so I wasn't sure I wanted to go that route.

The night of April 4th, myself and another black girl, the only ones in a class of white people, listened patiently as the patrol office gave us lessons on being good drivers. I didn't know the other young lady, I could only tell you she was uppity. She talked about her mother and her mother's bridge partner. She sat correct. I mean she crossed her legs when she sat and was very poised. She wore glasses, was tall but petite. She had large eyes and somehow, I felt intimidated because I had never met anyone like her before. Actually we never spoke, we did not really meet because she never actually talked to me directly. She sounded like a White Girl. I never knew anyone who sound like that nor spoke with her words crystal clear. After, we settled into our class mostly waiting for a break, another officer walked in and whispered in our instructor's ear. The instructor turned beet red almost speechless, then he paused, cleared his throat and announced. *"Ladies and gentlemen, I am here to informed you,"* and he paused. All eyes were on him, *"Dr. King has just been shot. We asked that you call your parents to come get you or leave now."* This class is dismissed until further notice.

"Oh My God! Someone screamed!"

Pandemonium. More screams of disbelief. White people were falling over the chairs trying to get to the door. I was in a daze.

"God help me! Dr. King has been shot!"

I heard others scream. I began to feel terrified. I had no way of calling my Mama. No idea of how I might be getting home, or whether I would be killed trying to get there. Were white people shooting up black folks? They had the nerve to shoot Dr. King. I just knew my black ass would be next. I did not want to die. I remember shaking so hard. Nobody offered to take me home. I thought I heard someone say that the telephone lines were down. Then this black man, the father of this uppity girl asked *"Where do you lived? Where do live?"* He shouted! *"I uh, I uh, live in SOUTH MEMPHIS ON MICHIGAN STREET"!* He asked again *"WHERE DO YOU LIVE?"* He shouted again. I thought that I had answered him but then I gave him my address *"1296 MICHIGAN STREET, OFF PARKWAY AND THIRD!"* He said *"I know where it is, let's go!"* His voiced was hurried and frightenedl. *"DUCK DOWN!"* he screamed. *"GET IN THE BACK AND DUCK DOWN AND COVER YOUR HEADS AND DO NOT LOOK UP"!*

He leaned to the right toward the passenger seat with his left arm on the steering wheel but he never sat straight up to make his head visible for any stray bullets. We could hear gun shots and sirens. He would peek up every now and then to drive where we would not have an accident. But he was dodging and ducking his head. *"How fast was he going? I don't know. How long did it take us to get home. Seem like forever?"* We could hear more sirens, then guns shots. It was awful. It was awful. We finally made it. He stretched his arm across the back seat to unlatch the back door where we had been lying on the back floor. He pushed the door out really hard and urged me to ***"Run! Run!"*** I awkwardly slid out of the car, shaking, crying and hoping I wouldn't get caught by a stray bullet. I didn't want to die on my doorstep, on the front porch in my own neighborhood.

I dropped to the bottom of our concrete steps and crawled up to the top screaming all the way ***"Mama! Mama! Open the Door! Open the Door!"*** Scratching at the screen door, she opened and looked out but not down at me on the porch. Her eyes shifted and fixed immediately on me laying on the porch and she shouted, "**Look up girl and get out of the way.**" I did not realize that I was blocking the screen door preventing her from opening it. I made it in the house. All of the lights were out except the light from our black and white television of the news. The dreadful news that Dr. King had been killed. My Mama never asked how I got home. Everyone was crying. Dr. King is dead. Dr. King is dead.

NEXT DAY

Erie. My Mama of all things wanted to go to the fabric store. We were we on curfew. Everyone had be off the streets by 6 pm and in their homes by 7 pm and she wanted to go Joann Fabric in Frayser! The Frayser area at the time was taboo for black folks. We knew not to be in Frayser because you were not going to see anyone that look like yourself. Frayser was off limits. However, in 1968, you did not question your Mama when she said lets go. No questions ask. We did not know how the climate would be in the store. It was quite empty. A scatter of white people here and there. Not a black soul in sight. This white woman met us with a smile. A huge smile *"Can I help you?"* It was as if she was studying our faces. Studying is something my Mama would say when she is sizing up people. My Mama was jubilant, as if, she knew that this white woman had something to be sorry about. The killing of Dr. King was major and this woman was sweet as sugar candy. My Mama said "No," she knew what she was looking for. The woman said, *"Let me know if I can help you."* You could tell she had that look like, *"I don't want no trouble,"* get what you need and get the hell out. And we did. We were probably thinking the same thing especially since we had to go clean across town to get back to South Memphis.

****

We would purposely sit on the porch until the last minute. The army tanks would roll up and down our streets near time for the curfew. The soldiers would bellowed out on their bullhorns letting us know that it was time to go in. We would sit there to the last minute. *"ALL LIGHTS OUT BY 7 PM ALL LIGHTS OUT BY 7 PM!"* Yeah, not only did we have to be in at 6 pm but all lights in our home had to be out by 7 pm.

After the initial riot, in the Press Schmiter evening newspaper, there was a young girl standing in front of a historical store called A. Schwab. A. Schwab, a general store, had been around for over 100 years, Michaele's family was quite proud of her to have a cashiers job there, especially since she had a small baby around 9 months old. The horror on her face told the story of the devastation in the aftermath of a peace march gone awry.

Michaele's Story: My sister
"This part of the famed Beale Street was like a family. We looked out for one other. The unit was gone. Forever! It was like the rug had been ripped out from under us. The business family and community was gone.

The shattered glass and the stillness, clothes spewed in the middle of the street reminded me of something I saw on television, and not something I ever expected to experience. It was like a war zone. Broken glass. Broken lives. Broken faith. Storeowners left and didn't returned. The fear was a strong presence. I wondered about the future of this place. Seeing armor cars rolling down Beale Street. I never ever seen anything like this. On April 4th, I was standing at the bus stop when sirens blaring so loudly that I covered my ears, police cars zoomed past me and the others standing at Beale and Main Street. To my right, they sped on to a small side street off Main. Store owners began to close. Bewildered. "Whats going on," she said to herself. Then she heard a loud scream as she boarded the bus; someone shouted out 'They done shot Dr. King,' tears flowed down the rider's face. 'Somebody done shot Dr. King!!!' His shock and dismay turned to anger. He lowered his head and said it again 'somebody done shot him. Somebody shot Dr. King!!!!!'"

CHAOS, CONFUSION & CURFEW

In our neighborhood around this time, any other year, students and families would be getting ready for graduation, senior prom, state championships, Cotton Carnival and hanging out Saturdays downtown until the stores closed. But not this year. This was 1968, the year of:

Curfew

Martial law.
Off your porches by 6 pm.
All citizens had to be off the streets by 6 pm.
Army tanks with loud bullhorns.
All lights in your home off by 7 pm.
No football games.
No football games!!!!!!!
No milling around school.
Going straight home.
You could not stand around.
The soldiers stood guard in a long row at our school.
Guns ready to fired if needed.

*We had to walk in between the soldiers as we approached or left the school.
No milling in the streets.
I dare you to say anything to them.
In my head when I would see the one Black soldier. I wanted to ask, "How does this make you feel?" I dared not. I dared not.
I would not dream of asking him that but I did want to know.
No prom for the 1968 Class of George Washington Carver High School.*

To this day the 1968 Class is also referred to as the class with no prom. No prom! Something you looked forward to since you were a child and then junior high then high school and someone says no prom. Well they did not have an official year book either, so I heard. I believe that is correct...no prom...damn! I was still that giddy, silly young girl who dreamed of dances, handsome suitors and becoming grown.

"It is during our darkest moments that we must focus to see the light."
Aristotle

CHAPTER 12
ON THE STEPS OF CITY HALL

Standing there on the steps of Memphis City Hall, my body limp in anguish, almost disoriented, disappointed, sad, and in disbelief. My body literally numb. I have cried so much. It's cloudy outside. Standing on a cloudy day with a picket sign in my hand. Gloomy, the weatherman said rain, a sunny day was out of the question, but *"PLEASE God don't let it rain."* The grown folks were all taking their turns at the microphone; one by one they spoke of Dr. Martin Luther King, Jr. and how great a man he was. Was? Dr. King was dead...dead... dead...gone. Gone forever....STANDING IN FRONT OF City Hall, a place where we were supposed to have ended the day when Dr.

King showed up for the march. A march that was tragically stop never to be resumed because now he is gone. He is gone forever.

I stood there frozen zombie like then my eyes fixed on this incredible handsome, tall, stoic, dressed all in black this fine Man. His face stern like, his piercing eyes as hard as the steps planted on concrete. Yet somehow he glided across the pavement like a gazelle. His movements were fixed like his anger. He walked stiff and deliberate. He approached the crowd, spoke and as he exited the stage, he turned slighted to my left. A hundred horses were holding my words back. I wanted to scream but I couldn't. *"Take me with you is what I wanted to say. Please is what I wanted to say."* My eyes spoke loudly, but my words would not come as I turned my head and starred at the ground. I wasn't worthy. I looked up and to him. He looked off.

His friend of many years Dr. King had been killed; he was someone that had poured hundreds of thousands of dollars into Dr. King's mission and now he was gone and you could clearly see the anguish on his face. He appeared heartbroken in disbelief. The veins in his forehead met his brows with distain. I wanted to run to him, hug him, hold him, allow my body to melt into his chest, but I couldn't. I wouldn't dare. I clinched my fists curled my bottom lip over my top. I want to leave this place!!!!! I am a girl, a 16-year-old girl who had gotten herself mixed up in something far greater than I ever thought I would, but I could not move. I wanted to. I could not. My eyes followed him. His gaunt look as his trench coat floated softly in the windy breeze. He sailed slowly by; head held high with authority. In a swaggering way and long before the Barack Obamas, Denzel Washingtons and Wesley Snipes. He seemed to glide across the patch of grass, then he was gone. He disappeared into a waiting car. Trying to hold back my tears, I couldn't hold back. The tears overflowed as I tried to wipe them away. I wept, my eyes batting wildly. This man was Harry Belafonte, civil rights activist, superb actor, singer, father and a man devastated by the loss of his friend Dr. Martin Luther King, Jr.

Everyone was speaking of peace and non-violence. Crap! I felt so sorry for Mrs. Coretta. I made my way through the crowd until I stood front and center of the stage. Jesse Jackson, civil rights activist and one of Dr. King's right hand men spotted me, stretched his hand out to me and asked whether I wanted to join them on stage. I did. I was just a teenage girl in the audience of hundreds, nothing special, but I felt powerful on the stage that day looking over the heads of the many people that were there. Many faces of sadness and disbelief as others talked of peace. I heard the voices but I couldn't really feel anything. I wouldn't smile or nothing. I stood there like a black panther with my high afro and dark shades. Damn. Dr. King is dead...unbelievable. So what is the point?

Earlier that day we had reassembled in front of Clayborn Temple it was the first time for many of us since "The March" on March 28, 1968, when Dr. King showed up. When a bunch of fools disrupted the first march, threw rocks at cars, broke windows, and stole stuff that did not belong to them. Which in turn brought the police down on all the rest of us, sprayed with tear gas and beaten by the police, hemmed up in Clayborn Temple, thinking we were going to die. Here they are speaking of peace. Peace. Dr. King stated in his last speech *"I've Been to the Mountaintop"* at Mason Temple, that we *would* go out again and now he is dead. I am so sad.

    The day that he was murdered, he and his followers had been hit with an injunction. The night before, I listened intensely to my Mama's small radio to the roaring crowd chanting for Dr. King to come to speak. After showing up and speaking, I hung on his every word with thunder and lightning as the backdrop. The dark skies lit up with shrieks and shrieks of lightening. It was scary. I wanted badly to be there but my Mama said that I could only go, if Michaele, my next oldest sister would go along with me. Strangely, she was not forcing Michaele to go. All my Mama had to do was to tell Michaele that she was going with me. I remember that night; I could not understand why Michaele would not go along with me. She knew how badly I wanted to be there. I had participated this far, why stop now? This puzzled me for years. I could not understand why she would not go along with me. I found out why 40 years later, Michaele admitted that the reason she did not go was that she had sneaked out and made a called to her pastor, Bishop Gary Hunt to get his permission to go to the temple with me. Bishop Hunt informed Michaele not to go because Dr. King was a Baptist and being from an Apostolic church, this would not be a good mix. When Michaele confessed this to me, I could not say a word. I had never ever asked her why she didn't go with me and I could have accepted any reason but this one. Floored, I remember years ago, several members of my family would not visit my grandmother in Mississippi; because if they missed a Sunday of church, the pastor would chew them out. Going to my grandmothers on a Sunday was not an option. *"Can you believe such craziness?"*

    A fool cut him down on the balcony of The Lorraine Motel before we could march again. I was so ready to do it all over again and to get it right this time. This March would have happened if he had lived. This time we marched in silence. No talking or any singing folks dress in black. Tons of folks dressed in black. Mrs. King and other close to him were leading the march. This was not supposed happened. We carried our signs again. We took the same route, as we were to take the last time; only this time no one threw one bottle, not one piece of lumber like the 2 by 4 that had swished by my head during the first march. I do not remember seeing anyone cry. I guess our tears were buried deep inside or dried up from the shock of his death. I had to be there again. Nothing was stopping me this time! Then the speeches were over. It was so dark. **So Dark.**

"I alone cannot change the world, but I can cast a stone across the water to create many ripples."
                                            Mother Teresa

CHAPTER 13
HOW DID THE MARCH AFFECT MY LIFE?

June 4, 1968

I remember getting ready for bed. I am still 16-years-old. I will turn 17 on June 25 1968. I had a new beau and I could vote next year at 18. I was on the phone talking with my boyfriend, Lawrence Jones from Melrose High School. We both agreed that we would easily vote for Bobby Kennedy if we could vote. We lingered on the phone for hours, as the Democratic National Convention was taking place in California. Bobby Kennedy was giving his victory speech. Yeah I thought, I would vote for him as I dose off to sleep. In the middle of the night I was awaken by my niece, Audrey, shaking me as if she had gone crazy. He dead!!!...He dead! Bobby Kennedy is deaddddd Bobby Kennedy is dead was etched in my brain. I was in disbelief. Dr. King had just been killed, now Bobby Kennedy. He decided to run for president and now he is dead; shot down. This is some scary stuff. I could not believe what she was saying. *"Is this real? It can't be."* I was so sad. The very person that in one more year I could vote for was gone. No. These people have lost their minds. What is going on? Devastated over Kennedy's death, ready to give up living in America, mostly because of this terrible fear I now had of white people and the power that I thought that they held. I was just a scared teenager wondering what had happen to the world around me. I could not see myself giving up my life and someone not agreeing with me, wanting to kill me. I developed a fear like none other. I wanted to be invisible. No one had a recovery counselor to come and speak to us. No one ever asked me, *"what affect did this have on you?"*

You dusted yourself off and kept going. Others have died and who did I think I was. I felt like I was a nobody because if they kill Dr. King. My ass is grass. I adapted this saying in my head. *"I ain't shit. If they could kill Dr. King and Bobby Kennedy, who am I? I could be a fly on the wall. If someone smashed me, no one would care or even know."* The death of Dr. King compounded with Bobby Kennedy's death was enough civil rights bull for me. People will kill you. I was weak and dismayed. I could not understand the craziness of it all.

However, I soldiered on. Soon after, the SCLC was holding their annual meeting here right after Dr. King was assassinated and again I was asked to serve and if I knew others who would serve as host for the meeting that took place at a church on Parkway. I did and got some friends to participate too. Barbara Wooten, Hazel Scott and the rest I do not remember, but people like Jesse Jackson and Andrew Young of Atlanta were all guest speakers. I remember because it was another milestone or wake up call for me. We were giggling and acting silly like high school teenagers do. Hazel dared me to go up and asked Andrew Young for his autograph. I hesitated a bit. Maybe I should have followed my gut instinct and not done it but back then I wanted to be liked by the poplar girls. Hazel was popular, loud, could sing, was well connected, had a cute brother that sang with the Temprees, and they had let me in.

    I stalled and walked up to Mr. Young and mumbled can I have your autograph? I looked back to see Hazel snickering and punching someone on the shoulder, little did I know how bad I was being set up. He, Mr. Young shooed me off, he held up his hand with fingers spread with this frown yet welcoming face and said, *"No."* He paused, *"No."* Then he said it again. *"I'm no movie star. No."* I said, *"Thank you anyway,"* walking off disappointed, but she dared me and I did it, only to be met with great laughter from her and the crew of how I just got dissed. Andrew Young did not stop there, when it was his time to speak, he blasted us. **'Youths,'** but we knew he was talking about me, **"You** *need to read! We are standing on the shoulders of giants who have given up there lives that we are here today, he had that anger in his voice like 'wake up people!'"* I felt very small and I got the message my friends roared with laughter because they knew he was speaking to me. I felt so humiliated, yet I truly understood. How could I be so foolish? Dr. King had just been murdered and me wanting an autograph was ridiculous. I tried somehow in my mind at least to keep this strong awareness of doing the right thing; however, I was truly besieged with fear of the white man and what could happen to me if I got out of line. I mean I had see on TV how black folks were sprayed with water, bitten and charged by dogs, yelled at, and pushed around. Now I had been involved personally in a crowd of people and I saw first hand how things could get out of control and the consequences of an angry mob. I was scared and I did not want to die. I was only 16. What's the use of protesting or marching because if you speak out you will be taken out.

"We must adjust to changing times and still hold to unchanging principles."
Jimmy Carter

CHAPTER 14
MARRIED & PREGNANT BY APRIL 1969

As I mentioned previously, when I first heard his voice, he was being interviewed by a local radio personality. As he spoke his voice sounded much older than the age of 16 and I felt drawn to it. I listened and then realized that the boy that was speaking was the same football player who lost his leg during practice at the local high school. This was the talk around town and so at that moment I stopped and listened. He attended the same high school that I would be attending the following fall. He described the day his mother and father had to delivered the horrible news to him that the doctors would have to amputate his leg. At that moment I wanted to know him. I wanted to know the person behind the voice. I even got it in my mind that I wanted to marry him. I believe to this day that God did want me to marry Charles. I made up my mind that summer when school starts, I would look for him. I had his name, Charles but nothing else. I didn't have the slightest clue of how he looked nor how I would recognize him, but I was on a mission.

    I searched for him for over a year at Carver High School hoping to bump into him or hear someone call out his name. On campus, I would hear discussions from the upper-class jocks talking about the incident but no one ever referring to anyone near them named, Charles. The following year that opportunity came in the most awkward way. After being introduced by phone then formally, for several years, we were on and off again over the telephone. At times I would see him on campus after school hanging around talking to other guys. We would have small talk but nothing serious. As I grew older we kissed and did grinding, but I was to afraid to go all the way. I heard rumors that he had other girlfriends anyway. Lots of them. That and the silliness of being infatuated and lovestruck faded overtime during the spring of 1968. I was thinking of more serious things like Sanitation strikes, non-violent marches and helping my neighbors. I fluctuated between a silly girl interested in boys and making a name for myself on campus and doing something to right the wrongs I saw in my community.

Then something happened. Actually multiple things: I experienced the aftermath of a march turned to chaos, lived with curfews and soldiers with guns as I went to school and back home, saw many of the great men of the Civil Rights Movement killed and seriously thought I was going to die as well. I put on a good face or front, but I was terrified underneath. I never had a father and my older brothers were all off living on their own. I was looking for a safe place and not finding one. Then this once cocky guy began to call again. I was besieged with phone calls from

Charles day after day. I wasn't really interested in him anymore but he was older and I had cared about him and considered him a friend. His voice still touched me and gave me a sense of not being alone. He was relentless in his pursuit so I eventually gave in and said yes to the question *"Would you go with me?"* Young people that is decoded today as *"Hester would you be my girlfriend?"* Things began to escalate in our relationship. Heavy kissing and heavy groping. I turned 17 on June 25, 1968 and he was 21-years-old. I didn't dare tell my Mama his age. After all I was underage according to the law. If anything got out of hand it could be a problem. In December of 1968, during Christmas school break, it did get out of hand. And you guessed it, I became pregnant. Again I was terrified for anyone to find out, but of course they did.

  When my Mama found out things began to happen fast. A call was made to California to get my brother and sister to weigh in on a suggestion of giving my unborn child away or getting married! My sisters Ethel and Joyce suggestions were loud and clear GET MARRIED!! My Mama wasn't saying anything much to my surprise. I was shocked when my Mama suggested locking Charles up for statutory rape. I was a willing participant in my relationship with Charles and having him locked up was not in the cards. No way! I refused to talk to my brother Jerry who was stationed in Germany. My brother Royal and sister Dorothy's advice was unmentionable. But I spoke up loudly and said, *"I don't want to get married but I do want to keep my baby."* That statement didn't last long. My Holy Roller sister, Joyce who had gotten pregnant and married at 15, was adamant about the two of us getting married. After all we did not want to bring a "bastard child" into this world. Whew, talk about heavy.

    I was considering college and getting married was much too serious for me. Every day I avoided Charles' phone calls, however my dear sister would not let up. Every opportunity that she had she hounded me to no end about getting married. She had the scriptures to back up her claim that I shouldn't bring a child into this world without being married. I finally gave in and said yes to my sister, not Charles. She called Charles, and gave him the announcement that I said, *"yes"*. Then she said, *"now ya'll got to set a date!"*

The date was April 19, 1969, one year and twenty-two days since the day that I absolutely thought I would die and one year and fifteen days after my life was crushed when Dr. King was murdered. I lived in fear for too long to go through this madness by myself. Maybe, just maybe marriage isn't such a bad idea after all. At least I would have someone, unlike a father or brother to protect me. I somehow felt that it was Charles responsibility to be the father that I never had; to protect me from the ills of society. A tall order to say the least. I continued being that silly, giddy high school girl part of the time and then the rest of the time frighten to death of loud noises, crowds and avoiding all heated arguments and confrontations. This behavior of course spilled over into the marriage. After hearing this boy being interviewed on a local station and believing God meant for me to be his wife (I was only 11 years old thn). Years of denying my love for him, I concluded if I loved him once I could love him again. Funny how life works out, the day that my dear friend Ike and my sister Michaele took me to visit a so called friend, and witnessed the two of us kissing passionately, was the same man that ended up my husband for 23 years.

I know now that I had a lot of unresolved issues due to the trauma of my early years and participation in the Memphis Sanitation Strike of 1968. I recently shared with Charles despite everything that happened, I am glad we have 2 handsome sons, daughter-in-laws and 5 wonderful grandchildren. I am at peace with that part of my life now.

WHEN I SAW IKE AGAIN

I never saw my friend Ike again until after I was married. He never came back around and I was too chicken to walk around

Willie Jackson house to ask him about Ike. I assumed that Ike had left to return to Mississippi. Standing on Beale Street, waiting to catch the bus with my little baby in my arms I saw this person that I thought I recognized. Oh goodness it's Ike Simpson. I stood back as to not let him see me but it was too late. He saw me; walked over and asked whether that was my baby. *"Yes"* I said. *"How are you?"* I asked. *"Fine, hows is you?"* he asked. *"Fine, I'm married,"* I blurted out. Ike said, **"Married?"** He was shocked and surprised. He paused and shook his head before he spoke again. *"Tell me something lil gurl, that guy that I took you over to his house, please tell me that ain't who you married is it?"* What could I say, but **"Yes."** He walked off shaking his head, *"You mess me up lil gurl, you mess me up."*

    I saw Ike one more time years later and he had become a musician. I was not surprised as he had the most beautiful voice. However, I was quite surprised when he told me that he had written a song about me. He game me a copy of *"I'm In Love With Somebody That's IN Love With Somebody Else."*

"Every great dream begins with a dreamer, always remember, you have within you the strength, the patience, and the passion to reach for the stars to change the world."
Harriet Tubman

CHAPTER 15
NO PROM

I was graduating the next year 1969. As much as I anticipated that prom, I could not go, I was pregnant by December 1968, married the following April and had a baby in September of 1969 and that was it. I wanted to go, I really did. But someone said how in the heck is a pregnant, married woman going to go to the prom. In the truest sense of the word, I really was not a woman yet, but I was married. In my mind and heart, I was still just a silly, fearful girl.

No prom celebration for Mrs. Hester Moore, but I was able to participate in graduation ceremonies. My Mama didn't come to my graduation even though she didn't have to work that day. *"It wasn't important,"* she said. *"People graduate every day."* She treated my graduation as she did the birthdays; we never received anything for our birthdays *"Folks had birthdays everyday"* she would say, *"People are born everyday and that ain't nothing special. Plus you is married, that ain't my responsibility. Let your husband be there."* She always said, *"She didn't have time to miss work."* We knew what that meant, the older sisters and brothers had that chore. Meeting with the teachers and then reporting to Mama.

    After I was married, People United to Save Humanity (PUSH), run by Jesse Jackson's headquarters came to our city at Rev. Kyles church, Monumental Baptist, I sat in the very back. He went on and on about helping and keeping the dream alive. He sounded convincing but I could not or refused to feel anything. I was married by then, had a baby and was miserable. *"Why am I in this world and what does it matter?"* were the questions I asked myself many times. I felt like what place could I go and not be afraid of white people. *"If I spoke up or out I could be killed. They killed Dr. King. Who I am? I am nothing."* I used to say to myself over and over: I am just a fly on the wall and someone can just come and smash me and no one would know or care. They killed Dr. King and Bobby Kennedy. I remember saying to myself, *"Why did Dr. King have to die and why here in Memphis of all places. Why here? Why here?"* When Bobby Kennedy was killed, I truly felt like if you were a Negro or Negro lover, fighter for civil rights, your ass was gravy.

    I could not see myself any longer, as someone willing to give up my life because others were willing to take my life if I got out of line. I was terrified but at the same time, for years, I felt depressed that I did not do enough. Too much violence had taken place over individual's rights and people were willing to kill because of it.

*"Spread love everywhere you go,
Let no one ever come to you without
leaving happier."*
Mother Teresa

CHAPTER 16
1998 – 30 YEARS AFTER

One of my theater professors, a white instructor Eastern Hale, had an assignment for me. I was taking an instructional technical class from him at Southwest Tennessee Community College. We were to meet in the control booth. As I approach him to get my assignment for the class, he was reading the *The Tri-State Defender*, the black newspaper, about the 30 years of Commemorating Dr. King's death. The National Civil Rights Museum had opened in 1991 and this was a very special historical occasion for Memphis. I quietly said to Mr. Hale that I had, *"participated in the 1968 march"* but *"I didn't like talking about it."* He asked, *"Why?"* My answer was, "Why? It still hurts in my soul...I did not need to recant that day. I did not need to relive that night when I was stranded at the driver's education building. I married the very next year, had a baby and just did not see any point in speaking up or out. How would it do any good." Then Mr. Hale said something that would forever change my life. "Well if you don't want to talk about it, write about it, put your story down on paper." I claimed, "It is too painful." He replied, "Write about the pain." I refused. Then he said, "This is your assignment for this semester; your writing will depend on that grade." Now this had absolutely nothing to do with technical theater but he had given an assignment and what was I to do. He also requested that he would like to see a progression of this writing each time I would come to class. "What could I say?" I asked him. He simply said, "Tell your story. Just tell your story."

I began to write something down every day and every word was fresh in my memory. After two weeks of writing, he added and additional request to the assignment. Contact the local newspapers; let them know we are looking for others with stories of their experiences during the 1968 Sanitation Strike. Have the letters sent here and we will contact these people later. We will review the letters and create a forum, a venue for them to talk. I did as he requested and the floodgates open. The sadness began to pour in.

    I don't remember all the letters but later we would meet some of the key players like Taylor Rodgers, who was the union rep and several sanitation workers. One in particular, I shall never forget, I do not remember his full name, a Mr. Williams. We talked on the phone and he requested that I read his letter. He had extreme arthritis in his back from the years of carrying the garbage cans on his shoulders, cans with holes of running sludge. The filth and slime running down his back. Flies followed him as he discarded the waste on dirty smelly trucks; only to do this over and over again. There were no plastic bags to protect him, no curbside pickup. Mr. Williams was unable to attend the meetings. His pain was too much so he asked me to speak for him; to read his letter. Much of his letter broke my heart, this man not having the right to speak out on such a bad job practice. He cried many times to me over the telephone about having to provide for his family, smelling of rotten sewage and receiving pay so meager that he had to apply for welfare.

Then there was Queen Aqua, a stout black woman from the hood of North Memphis. She always spoke as if she is giving a speech. Her head tilted upward from her short body. She was draped from head to toe with African attire; her voice filled the room. Herself a freedom fighter, she often talked about being soldiers in the civil rights movement. She talked on and on about the struggle, the players in the movement, the assignments, and the freedom fighters. She assured us that it was like running an army of soldiers to do the work. Someone had to do the work. She referred to me as a young soldier in the wilderness trying to find myself.

There was only one white in this group, a slightly overweight soft-spoken homemaker whose husband was the police chief in

Germantown in 1968. Germantown was a suburb of Memphis where mostly whites lived. Honestly, I was surprised that she showed up. I never expected a white person to be a part of this panel unless he or she had a key role in the movement but she was brave enough to show up and we welcomed her. I forgot her name but did not forget her story. Her family was vacationing in Arizona when the news of Dr. King's death hit. She was embarrassed to be from Memphis. People stopped her on the streets of Arizona when they saw her license plates. She hung in on the meetings until we had the actual panel discussion that was never was.

Charles Cartwright, the leader of The Truvaders, agreed to sit on the panel to discuss that period and hear the stories, but strangely the college had a power outage that evening. Cartwright was never given an opportunity to speak. We all had to evacuate the theater where the panel discussion took place. Oddly, he said to me that he was not surprised that similar occurrences had taken place several times before. In the past, when he was about to speak, the speaker system went out, a fire drill took place or the panel discussion was interrupted for another unknown reason. *"The public does not want to hear what I know or what I have to say."* said Cartwright. I never asked him to explain. He died some years later.

If not for Eastern Hale's technical class and him reading the Tri-State Defender newspaper and encouraging me to tell and write my story I probably never would have done it.

It took almost 30 years for me to talk about my experience during the 1968 Sanitation Strike.

In 2013, I considered writing a book and in 2017 the first edition of my book *"16N68: My Story"* was published.

"Get in good trouble, necessary trouble, and help redeem the soul of America."
John Lewis

CONCLUSION
THE IMPORTANCE OF TELLING OUR STORIES

True story, I personally met Maya Angelou at Rollins College in Winter Park Florida, a suburb of Orlando. I pushed my way through the crowd to say to her of all things that I loved to write poetry, however, I didn't like sharing my works. Well you can imagine the licking upside my head I received from the great Dr. Angelou, she said in her great melodious voice. *"Then you are cheating the world. God gave you a gift and it ain't for you to keep."* "Yes, ma'am," were my only words to her as she made her way through the crowd. I stood there reflecting on her massive body and powerful words. However, I still waited 30 years before I could share this story.

Even 30 years later the pain was still there. I did not want to talk about. I didn't visit anything that had to do with anything concerning the riot, civil rights, or Dr. Martin Luther King, Jr. It hurt too much. I could still smell the mace when I would talk about it. The fear was still in my soul. And why would anyone want to talk about something so dreadful.

After I audition to become a teaching artist for the Memphis Arts Council, Tracy Ford and Amelia Barton, both white women, offered to assist in developing a one-woman show to present to the Memphis City Schools.

Now that was a tall order. My first school would be Westwood High School. I felt like these students were going to eat me alive, but they were quite receptive to my story. They listened with intense looks on their faces.

After the performance, students rushed to the stage, most were crying and thanking me for sharing my story. Some wept openly and said this was the first time anyone ever came and told them the truth about what really went on. Well this was my truth of my experience. Anything that happened behind closed doors with the organizers, I had no way of knowing. I am only speaking from my view, my experience, my fear, my anger, my grief. I was scared and thought that I was going to die that day of the ill-fated march. I thought that my Mama would not know where to get me. That day that we were hung up in the church, I surely knew that the police would storm in shooting anything that moved.

I had no idea that I would be speaking or writing a book. I never thought that I would turn 17 or 18 or 19 or even 20. I walked around for many years often thinking that I should have done more. I often thought who in the hell did I think I was to think that I could make a difference. People gave their lives and I was not willing to do so. I had no reason to complain, I am a nobody in the movement, in the scheme of things. I had no way of anybody even remembering who I was. And what did I do but hold a damn sign and walk in the day and night in front of stores singing songs like *"We shall overcome, and I ain't gonna let nobody turn me around."*

I thought as a child and I responded as a child. I had no one to wrap their arms around me and say, *"You did what you did when you did it. One makes one hundred, it took one of me to make two and so on and so on."* Well this sounds all good and stuff but I was an emotionally wreck for years. I could have done more; I often said to myself, I should have died. Should have laid down my life like some of the others. It was terrible for me to think that I was thinking of dying and I did not want to die. I was scared. I walked around for years hating white people, because a white man killed Dr. King. A white man killed Bobby Kennedy (or the system which is white killed them). I don't know. I can see that my life did not mean a thing, even to talk about it. Why would I? So many others were there, why am I writing or even talking about it. Now I see that all our stories matter. That's why I continue to tell my story and encourage others to tell their stories.

In Vancouver Washington, Madison and Toma Wisconsin, Orlando Florida, Memphis Tennessee, Richmond Virginia, Greenwood and Byhalia Mississippi, Caruthersville, Missouri, Dallas, Texas and everywhere, I have spoken, the first question students ask is *"Did you see him, did you see Dr. Martin Luther King,"* and the answer is always the same, "No." If you want me to stir up my story again, retrace my steps, conjure up all those emotions and re-smell the mace, every smell that caused my eyes to burn like hell. I will talk about that, but I won't lie and say I stood next to Dr. King, we were all in the march together.

Chance encounter: I was at the Civil Rights Museum telling my story to a group of students. I noticed a worker at the museum come in. She paused, a white woman with papers in her hand. She stopped, looked over at me and stared, I thought maybe she wanted to speak to me or maybe she was just interested in what I was saying. As I spoke, she adjusted her glasses with her left hand, she waited, still staring at me, when I was finished, she walked over to me quietly and said to me, "*I was there that night.*"

I said. "*Where?*" She said, "*I was there that night at the driver's license place I was in that same room that night.*" I asked, "*You were there?*" She said. "*Yes.*" I said to myself, *how could she be?* I really did not what to say that. I really wanted to break down but I could not. What I realize was this is not my story alone. Somehow I felt like an invisible body to the 100's of others who stories had not been told. My pain is my pain all by myself. Her pain belongs to her. I didn't bother to get her name. I did not care; somehow, I felt that I owned this particular part that needed to be told. She reminded me that I didn't. I felt like she couldn't imagine what I had gone through. Yet I had no idea what she had gone through as if it didn't matter and it does.

Like an empty vessel no muscles in my body to get by I am weak.
I cry.
I ponder and wonder when I am going to die.

I am nothing.

Do you know how it feels to feel like nothing?

Like you are not important.

They done killed Dr. King.

They done killed Bobby Kennedy.

Who am I?

How is a man of statue measured? By his deeds? His works? His character? His intellect?

Then do the others matter who come from the depths of ignorance are they to be ignored?

His soul cries out to like souls of any man the kings stripped naked of what has been bestowed to him. How would you know his statue if those stripped naked stood side by side.

No words spoken to say the difference. All of you come naked into the world.

Only when we wear the clothes of the assigned character that we deem ourselves, Do we become Different.

This is not my story alone. I only own my portion.

FOR THE PEOPLE WHO SHARED ADVICE OR WORD ENCOURAGEMENT I THANK YOU

Pastor Morris Henderson
Dr. Shaquille O'Neal
Little Richard
Marian & Wesley Snipes
Dick Gregory
Hattie Jackson
Dr. Willie Herrenton
James Meredith
Larry Morris
Charles Evers
Jimmi Langemo
Dreya Morrigan-Layman
Judson Memorial Church
Rev. Johnson E. Saulsberry, Jr.
Beverly Robinson
Maya Angelou
31st Street Baptist Church
Family and Friends

SPECIAL ACKNOWLEDGEMENTS

I dedicate this book to Mr. McGee, neighbor, father, brother, husband and Sanitation Worker.

Mr. McGee's daughter, Wilma. You truly have been a blessing. You gave me information that only you could give. I thank you so very much. The many times that I've called, you were always so giving.

Jerry Myles Johnson, 1962 graduated of Carver High School, brother, educator for 42 years, coach, Sunday school teacher, former slave (his words), son, and proponent of education. Education, education, education.

George Hunt and Irene Davis teachers of George Washington Carver High School for inviting me to participate in the marches of the Memphis Sanitation Strike.

Mary Joyce Johnson Wilson, my sister, minister, mother, retired captain, taught me to read and write. She beat my knuckles many times to get it right!

Vivian Stewart, Librarian, Southwest Tennessee Community College always encouraged me to keep going and share 16N68: My Story.

The most important men in my life, my sons Ahmad and Jabari. Their father, Charles once said, *"Hester you should be a writer."* I didn't believe him then. Thanks for encouraging me. Without him there's no them!

SPECIAL THANKS!!!!

Eastern Hale, Technical Professor at Southwest Tennessee Community College for threatening me nicely that my grade depended on my writing my story.

The Colony Library, Carrollton Library, and Lewisville Library were I spent many hours research and writing my book.

The Colony Writers Group, The Colony Texas for supporting and encouraging a new writer.

The Colony Senior Center where I spent many hours on the computer.

Professor Gray Matthews of University of Memphis.

Memphis Arts Council: Tracy Ford and Amelia Hart for giving me the opportunity. My first presentation of 16N68: My Story.

Mrs. Cagle of the Caruthersville School District for believing in me with the 16N68: My Story Presentation and Workshop.

To all the schools that gave me the opportunity to come and tell 16N68: My Story.

Shonedra Redd at Lewisville High School for giving me the opportunity to facilitate 16N68: My Story workshop and presentation. My first in Texas.

Rev. Johnson E. Saulsberry, Jr (Retired) of the April 4th Foundation for the work he does with the youth. Inviting me each year to facilitate the Civil Rights Workshops at Lemoyne–Owens College, in Memphis, Tennessee.

To all the students and adults that have heard my story, I hope I was able to move you to tell your story.

Ms. Hattie Jackson, Retired Principal of Memphis City Schools and wife of Reverend H. Ralph Jackson one of Dr. King's advisors for including my story in her book "16 Days Reflection".

Thank you Elaine Turner, Heritage Tours for recommending me to tell my story to ABC.

ABC Special: "Two Kings of Memphis" with Peter Jennings. Thank you for allowing me to tell my story nationally.

To the 1968 Class of George Washington Carver High School I appreciate you and that you stood up and out. God Bless.

To Judge Ernestine Hunt Dorse. We met during the Civil Rights training at Clayborn temple at 15 and 16. Here we are today. Thank God! More than 50 years later.

HESTER JOHNSON MOORE

I had no ideal that anything of this magnitude would happen as a result of participating in the 1968 Sanitation March to City Hall. This was the day I knew I was gonna die, I wouldn't live to see my 17th birthday and *"my Mama ain't gonna know where to find me!"*

As an actress, youth mentor, and storyteller, Hester shares with youth and adults her experiences as a 16-year-old girl during the Civil Rights Movement, Marches to Support the Sanitation Workers Strike, Dr. Martin Luther King, Jr. coming to Memphis to support their efforts, the death of friends, political activists and more during the late 1960's. She also performs one woman plays along with sharing the stories of many sheroes of the past, women like Harriet Tubman, Sojourner Truth, Phillis Wheatley, Fannie Lou Hamer and Congresswoman Barbara Jordan.

To request her One-Woman Shows, Civil Rights Workshop or reading of her book for your school, church, or organization email:

StoriesbyHMoore@gmail.com or HesterJMoore@gmail.com.